The
Mercian Maquis

The Mercian Maquis

The Secret Resistance Organisation in Herefordshire and Worcestershire during World War II

by
Bernard Lowry and Mick Wilks

LOGASTON PRESS

LOGASTON PRESS
Little Logaston, Logaston,
Woonton, Almeley, Herefordshire HR3 6QH

First published by Logaston Press 2002
Reprinted 2007, 2012
Copyright © text: Bernard Lowry & Mick Wilks 2002
Copyright © photographs: the authors unless othewise stated 2002
Copyright © drawings: Mick Wilks 2002

ISBN 978 1 873827 97 0

Set in Times by Logaston Press
and printed in Great Britain by
Bell & Bain Ltd, Glasgow

*Cover illustration: Dinmore railway tunnel mouth,
a potential target for demolition by Abednigo Patrol*

The authors dedicate this book to all Auxiliary Units and Special Duties personnel who trained so hard in anticipation of the invasion that never happened and who, until recently, have received so little recognition for what they were prepared to do.

Foreword to the 2007 reprint

Since *The Mercian Maquis* was first published in 2002, further research into Home Guard records formerly held by the now defunct Army Medal Office at Droitwich, has revealed that there were two other Auxiliary patrols in Worcestershire: at Malvern and at Evesham. Both were short-lived and the patrol members were not recorded in the 1942 Nominal Roll held by the National Archive at Kew. Further evidence has also come to light for the urban resistance organisation in Worcester and provides an explanation for the Auxiliary-like Operational Bases identified earlier, in and around the city. It is now clear that the resistance net organised in Britain in anticipation of a German invasion was much wider than previously thought and also included Home Guard guerrilla units that were organized in Worcestershire, against the prevailing government advice.

Further details of this more recent evidence can be found in the *The Defence of Worcestershire and the southern approaches to Birmingham in World War II*, also published by Logaston Press. However, this reprint of *The Mercian Maquis* has been made due to popular demand and to provide a background for the more recent research.

Contents

Acknowledgements

It has been a great privilege for the authors to speak to surviving members of the Auxiliariy Units who have between them provided a great deal of first-hand information on the methods of their recruiting, location of their operational bases (OBs), arms and equipment, training and so on. The paucity of primary documentary material on Auxiliary Units in general meant that direct interview with survivors was the only means of obtaining much of the information set out on the following pages. We therefore thank wholeheartedly the following former Auxiliaries: John Barker, Dr Tony Barling, John Boaz, Chris Bullock, Geoff Devereux, Jim Griffin, Tom Harwood, Joe King, 'Dick' Mayo, Geoffrey Morgan-Jones, Dick Philips, Horace Phillips, Roy Robinson, Ron Seymour, John Thornton, Harold Wilkins, Peter Wright and John Wythes. The late Colin Curnock, Jim Holt, 'Fred' Mayo and Basil Tadman all helped us with our researches before they passed away. We are extremely grateful for the opportunity to speak to them.

It is now over sixty years since the first of the Auxiliaries were recruited in the summer of 1940. Inevitably a large number of them, in fact the majority of them, have passed away, so we must thank members of their families for their contributions of memories, sometimes limited due to the secrecy surrounding their husband's, father's or brother's activities, but nevertheless important, and for contributing or allowing us to copy surviving documents, manuals and photographs. These are individually acknowledged where reproduced. These contributors are Joan Bemand, Jill Bertheaux, Adrian Chambers, Mrs Cleland Snr, David Cleland, John Fernihough, Mrs Andrew Green, Shirley Marler, Mrs C. Morris, Mary Morris, Mrs J. Potter, Bill Potter, Denise Sainsbury, Ruth Tadman, Geoff Thomas, Peter Turner, the family of Reg Wilkinson, Mrs S. Workman, and Pamela van Moppes.

A number of parallel and, in some respects, even more clandestine organisations were formed in 1940 onwards to supplement or carry out similar operations to those of the Auxiliary Units. We have gained a limited insight to these and for this we have to thank Edwina Burton for telling us of her experiences as a wartime ATS radio operator with the Auxiliary Units Special Duties Section, Bert Davies for telling us about his role as a radio mechanic, also with Special Duties Section, Geoff Gurney for recollections of his father's spying role in the Upton upon Severn area and George Vater for his anecdotes and written contributions on the courier message carrying and radio system in Monmouthshire. A former member of the Birmingham Home Guard contacted us as a result of the publicity given to our research and, while wishing to remain anonymous, gave us a valuable insight to the recruitment of urban Auxiliaries and his special training for 'X Branch' in the Birmingham area. Similarly, a former Worcester postman, who declined to give his name, told us that he and a number of his colleagues were recruited as couriers for the Auxiliaries in that area.

For some years now Dr William Ward has been coordinating research nationally on the Auxiliary Units for the Defence of Britain Project. He has been most helpful to us with background information to these organisations. The British Resistance Museum at Parham, Suffolk produce a newsletter on the subject and have reproduced Major Oxenden's 1944 history and explanation of the organisation and achievements of the Auxiliaries. The volunteers who run this museum have also helped us with other background information and made us most welcome at their reunion of former Auxiliaries held on 2 July 2000 at Parham. This event also marked the 60th anniversary of the establishment of Auxiliary Units.

Colin Jones, the Worcestershire County Coordinator for the Defence of Britain Project, and the staff of the Worcestershire County Archaeological Service, led by Malcolm Atkin, have provided much logistical and moral support for the study of the local Auxiliary Units and we thank them for their contribution. We are grateful too for the proof reading skills of Malcolm Atkin, Colin Jones and Debbie Overton, and for their welcome comments on the content of this document.

Other organisations who have directly or indirectly helped us to make contact with former Auxiliaries or their families include the editors and reporters of the local media, most notably BBC Radio Hereford and Worcester and the BBC TV programme Midlands Today, the *Hereford Times*, *Malvern Gazette*, *Ross Gazette* and the *Worcester Evening News*.

We must also thank the staffs of the Public Record Office at Kew, the Worcestershire and Sherwood Foresters Regimental Office at Norton Barracks, and the two County Record Offices in Hereford and Worcester for their help in researching the more conventional military defences in the two counties.

Individuals who have also helped and contributed to the study include Eric Bayliss, John Bennett, Jim Colebrooke, Bob Cross, John Dando, Mr D.A. Davies, Suzie Elliot, Gerry Evans, John Guise, John Guy, Mrs Hallpike, Bryan Heatley, Odette Hitchcock, Peter Knight, Tony Lockwood, Dr A.G. Moncrieff, Les Moore, Jack Oliver, Brian Orme and the late Gerry Tysoe.

Finally we thank Andy Johnson of Logaston Press for help and advice in presenting our work and for publishing the results.

Foreword

Both of the authors have been researching 20th-century defence sites in the West Midlands region for a number of years, most notably those defences put in place to resist a possible and feared German invasion from June 1940 onwards. Some of this research work has focussed on the role of the Local Defence Volunteers, later the Home Guard, in creating and manning the anti-invasion defence infra-structure. There is still much yet to be discovered regarding the defence of the West Midlands but it is already clear from our studies that the area was far from being a defence backwater; quite the reverse in fact.

As part of the defences around the Severn Estuary and as a protective screen to the south and west of the main West Midlands industrial areas of Birmingham, Coventry and the Black Country, a clandestine organisation was recruited, mainly from the embryo Home Guard, and trained to carry out acts of sabotage against the German forces who, it was envisaged by the defence planners, might well attempt to capture the main armaments industries in these areas with armoured thrusts from the west or south-west. A number of former members of this British resistance organisation, officially called GHQ Auxiliary Units, are still alive and living in and around the counties of Hereford and Worcester. From these, and a few who moved away from the area, together with family members of those who have passed away, it has been possible to piece together a large measure of their story. Documentary records of the organisation are scant and so this has been a 'just in time' exercise, because most of the survivors are now in their eighties and even nineties.

A greater number of the Auxiliary Unit members have survived in Worcestershire and, because more information is available about their activities and the location of their Operational Bases, somewhat lengthier coverage is given to this county. On the other hand it has been possible to locate and copy all of the photographs taken of the Herefordshire Patrols at Stand Down in 1944.

The story is also one of 'what if' because, although the threat of invasion by the Germans in the summer of 1940, or again in the spring of the next year, seemed real enough to the defenders, we now know that Hitler's failure to overcome the Royal Air Force in the Battle of Britain and his subsequent decision to attack Russia in June 1941, made this less likely. As a consequence, the Auxiliary Units were not called upon to help defend their country. Nevertheless, the men who were recruited, all civilian volunteers, were quite prepared to give their lives, and endanger those of their families, for their country. In addition they spent many hours enduring strenuous and dangerous training so that they would be as ready as possible to carry out their acts of nocturnal sabotage against the invader. All were sworn to secrecy about their role and their activities. Many have now taken those secrets to their graves and it is only recently that the local survivors have felt able to talk about their role. We have attempted to tell their story, as we understand it, for the benefit of future historians.

It may be apparent that the style of writing varies throughout the account. This is inevitable where two authors collaborate, each writing different sections. We considered it to be more important that the information collected was fully recorded, whatever the style of writing.

There is no doubt a great deal more to the story than you will read in these pages, particularly about the spying and message relaying system which was part of Special Duties Section. Our evidence for this organisation is presently limited and it is hoped that by revealing what we know, it may help those people who were involved in this activity in the two counties, but who may still be inhibited by their former secret status, to come forward and tell us their story while there is yet time to record the facts for posterity. Please do not hesitate to contact the publishers, who will pass on any information to the authors.

The summer of the year 2000 saw the 60th anniversary of the recruitment of the first Auxiliary patrols. This was marked by a reunion of Auxiliers and Special Duties' people from all over Britain on 2 July that year. The event was organised by, and held at, the Museum of British Resistance, Parham, Suffolk. Anyone wishing to see artifacts and material relating to the Auxiliary Units would find a visit to the museum rewarding. There is also a small display devoted to the Auxiliaries at the Imperial War Museum in London.

The Fuhrer and Supreme Commander of the Armed Forces.
Fuhrer Headquarters.
16th July 1940.

<u>Directive No. 16.</u>
<u>On preparations for a landing operation against England.</u>

Since England, in spite of her hopeless military
situation, shows no signs of being ready to come to an
understanding, I have decided to prepare a landing operation
against England and, if necessary carry it out.
   The aim of this operation will be to eliminate the English
homeland as a base for the prosecution of the war against
Germany and if necessary, to occupy it completely.
   I therefore order as follows:
   1. The landing will be in the form of a surprise crossing
on a wide front from about Ramsgate to the area west of the
Isle of Wight. Units of the Air Force will act as artillery,
and units of the Navy as engineers.
   <u>The possible advantages of limited operations before the</u>
<u>general crossing (e.g. the occupation of the Isle of Wight</u>
<u>or of the county of Cornwall) are to be considered</u> from the
point of view of each branch of the Armed Forces and the
results reported to me. I reserve the decision to myself.
   Preparations for the entire operation must be completed by
the middle of August.
   2. These preparations must also create such conditions as
will make a landing in England possible, vis:
      (a) The English Air Force must be so reduced morally
      and physically that it is unable to deliver any
      significant attack against the German crossing.
      (b) Mine-free channels must be cleared.
      (c) The Straights of Dover must be closely sealed off
      with minefields on both flanks; also the western
      entrance to the Channel approximately on a line
      Aldernay-Portland.
      (d) Strong forces of coastal artillery must command and
      protect the forward coastal area.
      (e) It is desirable that the English Navy be tied down
      shortly before the crossing, both in the North Sea and
      in the Mediterranean (by the Italians). For this
      purpose we must attempt even now to damage English
      home-based naval forces by air and torpedo attack as
      far as possible......

...... The invasion will bear the cover name 'Seelowe'
(Sealion)......

signed ADOLF HITLER.

*The above extract from Directive 16 sets the scene for the succeeding pages
and the authors have highlighted, by underlining, that section of the Directive
which deals with the possibility of diversionary attacks on Britain. Such
attacks had been predicted by the British GHQ Home Forces for the South
Wales coast and the Bristol Channel, as well as Cornwall. These possibilities
led to the recruitment, in the counties of Herefordshire and Worcestershire, of
the resistance organisation described later*

CHAPTER 1
Historical Background

The élite force known as the GHQ Auxiliary Units or GHQ Reserve was one of the most secret and little known British fighting organisations of the Second World War.

The early years of the last century had witnessed the British Army fighting or being involved in a number of wars where irregular forces operated on either side. Two particular campaigns, with the Boers in South Africa and against the IRA, greatly influenced British thinking about guerrilla warfare, and especially the influence of intelligence gathering by or about these irregulars. In the First World War T.E. Lawrence and a band of Arab irregulars had led successful behind the lines operations against the Turkish army and particularly its railway supply system. Acts of sabotage against the railways paralysed the movement of Turkish troops and supplies.

Individual members of the Army, which included a Captain Colin Gubbins and General Ironside, both of whom would later play a leading role in the establishment of the Auxiliary Units, had also had experience of conducting operations in the ill-fated Allied intervention in the vicious Russian Civil War in 1919. The Russians had a tradition of partisan warfare going back to Napoleonic times and Bolshevik *otryadi* (partisan units) played their part in the Civil War and their successes would not have escaped the notice of the British officers. In the 1930s the Soviets established NKVD (internal security organisation) Destruction Battalions. A BBC TV documentary 'Inside Russia's SAS' made in 1999 included an interview with Ilya Starinov, an NKVD officer. He describes how, before the Second World War, the Soviets had established deep cover units equipped with caches of explosives and food; the battalion members would appear to be loggers or fishing crews. The training was put into effect when Soviet 'advisors' were sent to aid the Republican side in the Spanish Civil War and several successful sabotage operations were carried out. In one operation a Nationalist train, carrying airforce officers, was destroyed. The partisan spirit would be revived in the USSR during the Second World War when large bodies of armed men and women, established behind German lines,

1

would wage a cruel war against the invader. To what extent the British military authorities were aware of Soviet developments is not clear, but in the late 1930s two small British Military Intelligence departments, Section D and GS(R), the former dealing with the technical side and the latter with the theoretical aspects of guerrilla warfare, began parallel studies into sabotage warfare. Their officers included Lieutenant-Colonel Laurence Grand, Major John Holland RA, the promoted Major Colin Gubbins and a Royal Engineers Officer, Millis Jefferis. Jefferis was an explosives and demolitions expert. Their research led to the production of three pamphlets covering intelligence and sabotage: *The Art of Guerrilla Warfare*, *How to Use High Explosives* and *The Partisan Leader's Handbook*. These were never distributed in Britain but would be translated and widely distributed in enemy occupied countries. The research, closely followed by Winston Churchill, would, in April 1939, be regularised by the establishment of a new specialist department, MI[R]. This department plus Section D would, in 1940, form the basis of the Special Operations Executive, tasked, in Churchill's words, 'to set Europe ablaze'. The design of sabotage material and the organisation of intelligence gathering for home and resistance movements overseas were therefore already in hand when war commenced.

The fall of France in July 1940 left Britain exposed to invasion. The Army was in no doubt that they did not have the means of preventing an enemy landing. With a coastline of many hundreds of miles, British military resources were too thinly stretched. Once the invasion had taken place, hopes were pinned on the series of inland stop-lines established by General Ironside in the summer of 1940. Using natural and man made obstacles, they were designed to delay enemy mobile forces sufficiently to enable the home forces to throw the enemy back. Ironside's plan was that not only would frontal assaults take place, but the Wehrmacht would also be attacked by groups of men trained in both sabotage and intelligence gathering and operating *behind* the German lines. These were the men of the Auxiliary Units. The majority would be recruited from existing members of the newly formed Home Guard who would be given a full police security vetting before admission and would be sworn to the Official Secrets Act. Such was the seriousness of this oath that it is only in recent years that the few survivors have agreed to discuss their work.

Created under the auspices of GHQ Home Forces in July 1940 by General Edmund Ironside and led by the promoted Colonel Gubbins, the Auxiliary Units do appear to have excited Churchill's febrile imagination. A memo dated 8 August 1940 from Duncan Sandys of the War Cabinet to Churchill sets out the rapid progress being made in their establishment. At that stage, it was envisaged that the Auxiliers would operate within the framework of the recently established Home Guard, and would consist of specially trained men who would operate on the flanks and rear of the enemy. Particular targets would consist of tank and lorry parks, ammunition dumps, outposts and stragglers. In addition, some would be snipers. The other function of the Units would be to provide a system of intelligence to regular forces from behind enemy lines.

During interviews with surviving Auxiliaries in Herefordshire and Worcestershire, the authors have been made very aware that assassination of individuals was another function of the patrols. The victims would have included German officers, without whom the enemy troops would have been less effective, any members of the Auxiliers' own patrols who might compromise the security of his colleagues, members of the local population who might similarly threaten the security of a patrol, and collaborators. It is understood that lists of the latter would have been provided to the patrol sergeants by the Intelligence Officer or later the Group Leader, but the surviving Auxiliers are understandably tight-lipped about this aspect of their work.

The memo went on to say that each Unit would be under a selected leader and consist of not more than a dozen men only operating during the night. Recruits would come from the ranks of young farmers, gamekeepers, hunt servants and others acquainted with their rural locality. At a time when the Home Guard relied on requisitioned shotguns and clubs, the Units would receive rifles and grenades, plus the Thompson sub-machinegun when available (from the USA). The recently introduced plastic explosive, delay action fuses and incendiary bombs would be also be issued (see chapter 6). Selected Units would also receive wireless and field telephone apparatus for intelligence work. The explosives together with food supplies were being concealed in carefully prepared hideouts, known only to the local leader. The Units were clearly intended at this stage to have a rural base.

The enthusiasm for irregular units and warfare was a typically Churchillian response. However, Churchill had such a force as the Auxiliary Units in mind even before the fall of France. At a conference of the Supreme Inter-Allied Command in France on 11 June 1940 he had suggested to a horrified Marshal Pétain the continuation of the struggle in that country by guerrilla warfare. The suggestion was dismissed immediately by Pétain as he felt that it would lead to the destruction of his country.

The newly established Units would be controlled by 12 Intelligence Officers, who would choose their locations and personnel, distribute and conceal the stores, train the men in their use, and act as liaison officers between the Units and Military Commanders. In the event of invasion the Units would operate on general instructions or, if the situation permitted, on the orders of the local Commander. In addition to training given by the Intelligence Officer and a small force of regular troops, pamphlets on the use of explosives and guerrilla warfare had been produced. *The Countryman's Diary 1939* was, presumably, one of these: ostensibly a diary distributed by Highworth's Fertilisers, it was a handbook on the use of explosives. The cover also contained an 'in' joke: 'You will find the name Highworth wherever quick results are required'! 'Care of Highworth Post Office' was the postal address used by the Auxiliary Units Headquarters at Coleshill House in Wiltshire.

At this stage, no consideration had been given to the underground hides (the Operational Base or OB) designed and built in late 1940 and early 1941 as shelters for each group of men (the Patrol). In the summer of 1940 the Auxiliers would operate from their homes and presumably meet at a pre-agreed point for instructions and action. The 'Units' at this stage appear to have consisted of a small number of men. When the expansion of the force occurred the earlier Units would be renamed Operational Branch Patrols and be given an individual code name. These Patrols would then be formed into county Groups. The term 'Auxiliary Units' would henceforth form the name of the organisation rather than its sub-groups.

In addition to the sabotage and assassination activities, the Sandys memo also mentions the intelligence-gathering role of the Units. A separate Special Duties Section was formed in 1941 under the control of Major Petherick MP who was billeted at Hannington Hall, not far from his office at Coleshill House. The role of the SDS was to spy on the invader and pass information via specially designed radios to secret Royal Corps of Signals detachments. The detachments, later manned by members of the women's Auxiliary Territorial Service, operated from above ground control stations. These were given a cover by being referred to as weather stations. In the event of an invasion the detachment would operate from a nearby, carefully camouflaged, underground 'zero' station. From this, information would be passed to the Army Commands by radio via a carefully camouflaged aerial. Each control 'zero' station received messages from five or six outstations. It is not entirely clear, but it is believed that the Special Duties Section information did not find its way directly back to the Operational Branch except via the Commands. In other words, there was no overlap, apart from the fact that some Intelligence Officers did, at varying times, carry out duties in both branches.

The Special Duties Section was an extremely secret organisation: its members, apart from the Intelligence Officers, were trained locally and did not travel to Coleshill House for training. Messengers, who were often young men, were trained to observe and to collect messages from dead letter drops that were then passed to a further drop for collection by the radio operator (the 'outstation'). The operator was equipped with a radio designed and built at Coleshill House by the Royal Corps of Signals. The TRD set (the initials stood for 'Transmit, Receive, Dabbs — Sergeant Dabbs was the designer) was a small five metre waveband radio. Messages were sent over the air, and so communication did not rely on Morse. Time could thus be saved in training operators, whose operational lives, in any event, would have been very brief. The outstations were located in a variety of secret locations, for example behind an altar or in a golf club locker room. It was intended that each member of this organisation would be a separate cell, and should not know the identity of his fellow agents. It also seems likely that the Intelligence Officers, at least in the early stages, used a *nom de guerre*—the officer for Monmouthshire used the name 'Tommy Atkins' to disguise his true identity.

During their investigations into the role of the Auxiliary Units the authors have also found evidence that individual saboteurs were also recruited from the ranks of the Home Guard and trained to operate at night in urban areas. Unlike the Auxiliary Units, these men remained as members of the Home Guard. The role of one particular urban saboteur is discussed in chapter 10.

Following the successful creation of the Auxiliary Units, Gubbins would move in November 1940 from Coleshill to join the recently formed Special Operations Executive, eventually becoming the head of that controversial organisation. Gubbins was an ideal choice for this post. The cell-like Units, equipped with specially developed sabotage materials, would reproduce themselves in the clandestine European resistance organisations. Lieutenant-Colonel Major would take his place at Coleshill, to be followed by Colonel The Lord Glanusk in February 1942. Other members of the Units would move on and join SOE or élite forces such as the SAS. The actor Anthony Quayle, for example, then a young Intelligence Officer, would leave the Units and face an arduous but adventurous SOE assignment in the Balkans.

To all intents and appearances still a member of the Home Guard and wearing the uniform of that organisation, the Auxilier ceased to be subject to local Home Guard routine. Instead he was under instructions of his Patrol Sergeant, who in turn was under the orders of the Intelligence Officer and, later in the War, of his Group Leader. However, details of the officers, at least, would remain in local Home Guard records until the standing down of the Home Guard in the winter of 1944. To facilitate the movement of its members, those with cars were issued with a 'G' licence and special petrol coupons. To explain the presence of the coupons, a certificate signed by the Intelligence Officer was issued, to whom, or the local Chief Constable, any enquirer was to be directed, both of whom had been supplied with the bearer's car registration number.

The Home Guardsman's role would eventually become fixed as the defence of his locality. The Auxilier's strength was also seen to be his knowledge of his local area, and to this extent there was common ground between them. A Home Guard Instruction, Number 51, *The Organisation of Home Guard Defence*, issued in 1943 defined the role of the Guardsman: 'Through their intimate knowledge of the ground they will know where to strike. Through accurate observing they will know when. Through training they will know how. Observe, plan, strike, withdraw. Re-organise and repeat the process somewhere else'. Whilst written for regular Home Guard instruction, these words, with the addition of 'nocturnal' would also equally describe the role of the Auxiliary patrols. However, their methods of operation would be quite different.

In the southern and eastern coastal counties of England, in South Wales and in Scotland patrols were recruited mainly from the ranks of the Home Guard in the summer and autumn of 1940. It is believed that the majority of the patrols in the inland counties of Monmouthshire, Herefordshire and Worcestershire may have been formed in the latter part of 1940, although it is known that the Broadheath patrol was formed by August 1940. Whilst the coastal patrols were trained by Army units, the inland counties received their training at Coleshill House, the headquarters of the Units. The possible explanation is that the coast was well supplied with Army divisions awaiting the invasion. Western Command, covering Wales, the Midlands and North-West England, and with its headquarters at Chester, had in 1940 believed that the area was vulnerable to a German diversionary attack in the South Wales area as long as Eire remained independent of the British war effort. Once established, the Germans could then advance towards the Midlands using the Bristol Channel and the valleys of the Severn, Towey and Wye. Had the industrial heartland fallen, further resistance would have been rendered extremely difficult as much of the country's arms production was centred there. This is the likely explanation for the existence of the inland patrols.

In October 1942 it was decided by the War Office that Home Guard Identity Cards were to show the Battalion number or county. For this purpose, it was necessary to allocate a form of identification to the Auxiliary Units whose members were, ostensibly, members of the Home Guard. This was achieved by dividing the personnel into three GHQ Reserve Battalions, numbered 201, 202 and 203. The Hereford and Worcester patrols would come under 202 Battalion administered from York. This innovation had an immediate and noticeable effect on the appearance of the Auxilier in uniform, as beneath the normal Home Guard flash on his battledress blouse would appear the Battalion number and county on a khaki cloth backing. The 201st Battalion, administered from Inverness covered Scotland and Northumberland and the 203rd Battalion, administered from Reading covered the area below the Severn-Thames line.

Area 19 of the Auxiliary Units covered the counties of Worcestershire (Groups 1a and b), Herefordshire (Group II), Monmouthshire (Group III) and Glamorganshire (Groups IVa and IVb).

The first Intelligence Officer charged in the summer of 1940 with recruiting the county patrols was Captain John Todd. How Todd found the candidates is not clear, but the men in Herefordshire and Worcestershire were mainly in the farming community and, as many were running farms or were eldest sons, they were in a reserved occupation and ineligible for call-up for military service. The choice of farmers was a natural one: they knew their surroundings intimately, could shoot and were physically fit and resourceful men. Todd would firstly choose the patrol sergeants: they would then choose, under absolute secrecy, men for their patrols. In Herefordshire, for example, the patrol sergeants were all farmers apart from Martin Hooton who was a private schoolmaster employed by a school evacuated to Herefordshire from the south of England. It is possible that he had links with the Officers' Training Corps as the school is likely to have had such a body. Some movement in and out of the patrols took place during the war as men were called up or changes occurred in the command structure.

Once the invasion crisis of the summer of 1940 had subsided, the Auxiliary Units settled down to training, expanding the number of patrols and the establishment of permanent underground Operational Bases in readiness for the possibility of invasion in the spring of 1941. However, the German invasion of Russia in June 1941, Operation Barbarossa, gave further breathing space. The successes of the German armies in Russia and the anticipated fall of the capital, Moscow, in the autumn of 1941 led to a further flurry of activity in the Units as, should Russia be beaten, the likelihood of an invasion of Britain would again be apparent. The failure of the German winter offensives and, especially, the crushing Soviet victory at Stalingrad in 1942 indicated that a full-scale invasion would now be unlikely and the level of activity in the Units declined somewhat. The Home Guard and the Auxiliary Units continued to act as a potential deterrent to the possibility of German raiding or sabotage operations against the country, but as the war turned even more in the Allies' favour, the Units were used to test the security of vulnerable sites such as airfields and troop encampments.

The Operational Branch of the Herefordshire and Worcestershire Auxiliaries would, however, play a brief role in June 1944 before the Units were stood down. The possibility of German diversionary sabotage raids along the south coast of England following the invasion of France on D-Day, 6 June, led to the despatch of local patrols to the Isle of Wight to guard military installations. By the winter of 1944, the successful outcome of the invasion led to the decision to stand down the Auxiliary Units. A letter dated 30 November from Colonel Frank Douglas, Commander Auxiliary Units, to all members of the Operational Branch announced the order. It is likely that the Special Duties Section also received an identical order as they, too, were stood down in 1944.

On 26 January 1945 the Hereford Auxiliaries held their first Annual Dinner at the Booth Hall in Hereford. In Worcestershire at least one reunion dinner was held at the Shuthonger Hotel. The ending of the war, post war austerity and the need to get on with rebuilding Britain and returning to normality may have led to a wish on the part of the Auxiliers to put the past behind them.

The existence of this secret organisation was first revealed in August 1945 when an accurate description of the roles played by the Operational Branch and the Special Duties Section was disclosed to the press. Likened to the French Maquis, the report stated that they were controlled from an unnamed headquarters. The report in *War Illustrated* of 17 August 1945 is especially interesting as, in addition to its description of the Operational Branch, it mentions the shadowy Special Duties Section stating that it had

> thousands of members in ... the coastal counties, all prepared as civilians
> to report on enemy movements and activities by their radios, communi-
> cating with senior military headquarters ... few knew their neighbour
> members, and probably are entirely unaware even today that the farmer
> up the lane or the postman in the village was also a Special Duties man.
> Women, land owners, business men and labourers attained a high profi-
> ciency of wireless skill, including the use of codes.

Were the Germans aware of the existence of the Auxiliary Units? The great
secrecy surrounding their creation and operation, and the fact that enemy intelligence in this country during the war was virtually non-existent makes this
unlikely. There is, however, a possible and intriguing but tenuous connection. In
the dying days of the Third Reich, the existence of a secret resistance organisation, the Werewolves, was announced by the Reich Minister for Propaganda, Dr
Joseph Goebbels. Little is known about them, but what little information there
is makes it clear that there were similarities between the Auxiliary Units and the
Werewolves. Their members were carefully selected and provided with underground hides and stores, their mission being to commit acts of sabotage and
terror behind the enemy's lines. In July 1999 the newsletter of the Museum fur
Historische Wehrtechnik in Germany described the discovery of a cache of
sabotage material in that country. It is possible that the contents, most of which
appear to have come from captured SOE or OSS (Office of Strategic Services—
US equivalent of SOE) stocks, were destined for the Werewolves. Many of the
items would have been recognisable to the Auxiliaries: plastic explosive, time
pencils, incendiaries, tyre burster and clam mines. In the event, faced by the
overwhelming power of the Allies, the Werewolves could achieve little.

What fate would have awaited captured Auxiliary Units members and their
community in the event of a German invasion? The German planners of
Operation Sealion had drafted orders giving the occupiers the power to execute
any person found in possession of firearms or wireless equipment. Armed
insurgents behind German lines were to be dealt with 'with the utmost
severity'. There is ample evidence from accounts of atrocities in occupied
Europe that German forces would have shown no mercy. The well known
destruction and massacre of the village and population of Oradour-sur-Glâne in
France in June 1944 by the Waffen SS Division 'Das Reich' is one example:
but there were hundreds of lesser known Oradours in the eastern territories of
occupied Europe.

After 1945, the secret army was largely forgotten until the 1960s when
David Lampe's book *The Last Ditch* appeared. The book, which remains the
best description of the Units so far, proved popular but, once again, the subject
fell from the public gaze. It is only in the last few years that, belatedly, the role
of individual counties has been the subject of research.

CHAPTER 2
Local Intelligence Officers & Group Leaders

The role of the Intelligence Officer was firstly to establish the location of each Auxiliary patrol, to recruit suitable members, and to provide the arms and explosives for the allotted tasks. In addition, he had to train and to motivate his men and deal with the necessary administration required in the supplying of arms and equipment. His line of command was from Coleshill and, presumably, there would have been liaison with the relevant Army Command especially in the event of an invasion.

The first Intelligence Officer for Herefordshire and Worcestershire was Captain John Ellerman Todd. Todd also organised the Monmouthshire patrols, where he was apparently known as 'Sweeney', and may also have been responsible for the setting up of the Special Duties sections there. Before the war he had been a stockbroker with the London firm of Williams de Broë and was related to the Ellerman shipping line family. He is believed to have lived at Llanfihangel Crucorny in the Honddu valley above Abergavenny. Todd must have spent a busy 1940 and 1941 recruiting, establishing, motivating and training his patrols.

Todd made an indelible impression on those he met. Variously dressed as the country gentleman with a trout fly festooned tweed hat, or in a pukka officer's uniform, he is recollected by several surviving patrol members for his bloodthirsty exhortations. In fact some feel that in an earlier age he would have been a Bluebeard or a Captain Kidd. A recruiting ploy of his was to ply candidates with beer; those who had to leave early were 'out'. Another entertainment was to introduce the new plastic explosive by throwing it against a wall in the presence of his charges; without a detonator and primer it was harmless, but his audience may not have known this!

Each patrol in Herefordshire and Worcestershire was given a code name based on a biblical character, presumably to avoid using either a name that suggested a geographical location or the leader's identity. To use either would have compromised security. It is assumed that the choice of names was an initiative of Captain Todd.

Eye Manor near Leominster, Herefordshire, the wartime home of
Captain Christopher Sandford, Auxiliary Units' Intelligence Officer.
Sandford's office was in an outbuilding to the right of the main house.
From here he could keep in wireless contact with headquarters.
(Bernard Lowry, courtesy of Dr A.G. Moncrieff)

One of the 12 Intelligence Officers recruited in 1940, Todd was, in early 1942, transferred to Special Operations Executive to deal with aspects of the invasion of the island of Madagascar, where the Executive's role was to counterbalance the influence of the local Vichy French government before and during the invasion. Working from Durban, South Africa, Todd's role would be to arrange the surrender of the Vichy forces on the island.

Whether Todd stayed with SOE after the Madagascar operation is not clear, but in 1942 Captain Christopher Sandford, who had served previously in the Leominster Home Guard, took his place. Sandford had moved to the beautiful and isolated 17th-century Eye Manor near Leominster before the war, from where he ran a small publishing house, the Golden Cockerel Press. The Press produced high quality books, amongst which were editions of books written by T.E. Lawrence, and other editions featuring engravings by Eric Gill who also designed the Golden Cockerel typeface.

Sandford used the manor to store and distribute explosives and is believed to have had a small, presumably Regular Army, staff to administer the three counties and to act as his guard. A lorry and staff car were provided for their use. A small store building at the side of the house served as Sandford's office and a radio hidden in the roof of the building allowed him to communicate with Coleshill. The aerial for the radio was led up the side of a nearby tree. Whether this radio is an indication that Sandford had responsibilities in respect of Special Duties is not clear.

At a later date, possibly the summer of 1943, Sandford's place as Intelligence Officer was taken over by Captain Lloyd Bucknall RA. By August,

Bucknall had signed, as Intelligence Officer, authorisation 'chits' to enable Auxiliers to avoid disclosing the nature of their duties. A Public Record Office document, dated 26th October 1943, records a Captain Johnson taking over the Special Duties role from Bucknall, in addition to retaining his existing responsibilities in Glamorganshire. A month later Bucknall is recorded as being the Intelligence Officer Operational Branch Welsh Borders—an area which included Herfordshire and Worcestershire. Bucknall, a Devonian, is believed to have lived with his family at Holmer and to have been a Regular Army Officer at Bullingham Barracks, Hereford.

A further PRO document dated 18 August 1944 states that the number of Regular Army personnel in GHQ Auxiliary Units had to be reduced. This may have referred to staff at Coleshill rather than those in the field. This led to the withdrawal of the Intelligence Officers and their HQ staff although Group Leaders would remain in place. By this stage of the war, the prospect of any local enemy action was decidedly *passé*. Group Leaders would now take over the role of controlling the local patrols until they were stood down later in the year.

Group Leaders had been appointed from the local Home Guard, probably in early 1941, and before the first courses, organised for their benefit at Coleshill, were undertaken in March of that year. Up until that time it was expected that the individual patrols would have acted more or less independently with occasional contact from their Intelligence Officer. At about the same time as Group Leaders were appointed Lt-Colonel Major had replaced Colonel Gubbins at Coleshill and it is perhaps his influence which led to a policy change in the operation of the patrols. Henceforth Intelligence Officers were to operate in unison with the Group Leaders coordinating their activities and organising group attacks. Later Group Leaders were to organise local competitions between patrols in order to select the best patrol from their area to go forward to the national semi-finals and finals at Coleshill. Another role of the Group Leaders was to help their Intelligence Officer in the distribution of stores to the patrols under their control.

The two Group Leaders in Herefordshire were Captains Hall and Lacon, each controlling three patrols on the departure of Bucknall. Lacon appears to have had the more senior position as the Nominal Roll in the PRO gives his title as Area Group Commander, (the terms 'Group Leader' and 'Group Commander' appear to be synonymous) responsible for administration and quartermaster duties ('A' and 'Q').

John Hall, who lived at the now demolished Holmer Grange, is believed to have been connected with Watkins Pomona Cider, also of Holmer, and would have known many of the Herefordshire farmers through the purchase of cider apples for the business. It is believed that both his garden and business premises were used by patrols for training purposes.

Geoffrey Somerset Lacon was a member of the Kevill-Davies family, who had occupied Croft Castle until 1923, when the Croft family repurchased the

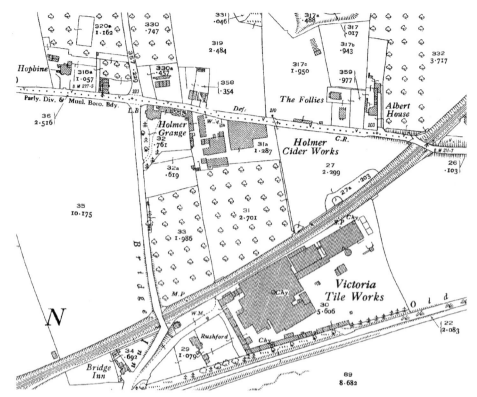

OS Map just before the Second World War showing Holmer Grange and the cider works. Where the lake that was used for training was located is not clear

property. On marriage, Lacon had taken the name of his wife whose family had property in Norfolk. It appears that he moved to Norfolk but returned during the war to reside at the large estate house occupied by his mother before the war and known as 'The Highwood' or 'Highwood House' on the edge of Bircher Common. Lacon is listed in the roll of the 1st Herefordshire (Leominster) Battalion Home Guard as a Lieutenant, commissioned in February 1942, this date possibly representing his move back to Herefordshire.

In Worcestershire, while the individual Auxiliary patrols would have initially acted more or less independantly with occasional contact from Captain Todd, there is some evidence that Thurston Holland-Martin of Overbury Court occupied a senior position in the local organisation. It is possible that he may have taken on the role of an unofficial group coordinator, in addition to his position as the initial patrol sergeant at Overbury.

There is, however, clearer evidence that two diamond merchants of Dutch ancestry, the van Moppes were more formally appointed as Group Leaders to administer the Worcestershire Auxiliaries, as early as 1941. The two brothers

Officers and NCOs of the Worcestershire Auxilary patrols, 1944. Left to Right:
Back Row: Sgt. John Wythes (Joshua Patrol),
Sgt Dick Philips (Claines Patrol), Sgt Alec Fernihough (David Patrol).
Middle Row: Cpl Ivor Thomas (Joshua Patrol), Sgt Basil Tadman (Overbury
Patrol), Sgt T.C. Dawe (QMS), Cpl Vincent Poland (Claines Patrol),
Cpl Harry Curnock (Davd Patrol).
Front Row: Sgt Val Clines (Samson Patrol), Lt Edmund van Moppes
(Group Leader), Capt Lewis van Moppes (Group Leader), Lt Roger Smith
(Group Leader), Sgt George Dalley (Jehu Patrol).
(Courtesy of John Fernihough)

were also members of the conventional Home Guard and are listed in 1941 as
Lieutenants in the 7th Worcestershire (Malvern) Battalion whose operational
area included Ombersley where they were now living. How and why the van
Moppes brothers came to be in Worcestershire, and to be responsible for the
local running of one of the most secret of our defence organisations is
intriguing.

A number of sources have told us that the two brothers were instrumental in
retrieving the stock of Dutch industrial diamonds before the invading German
forces captured Amsterdam in May 1940. Although a 'factional' account, the
book *Operation Amsterdam* does indicate the importance Winston Churchill,
who was then First Sea Lord, gave to obtaining the stock of industrial diamonds
in Holland, when the Germans invaded on the Whitsun weekend that year.

These commodities were essential to the armaments industry, and the means of spiriting away the one and a half million pounds worth, and the majority, of the diamonds from under the Germans' noses are well illustrated in the book. It is therefore believed that the van Moppes brothers were involved in this adventure, although their names have been changed in the book. The British Major Dillon referred to in the book was in fact Monty Chidson, an MI6/SIS agent, who planned the detail and coordinated the 'raid'. All three escaped from Amsterdam only half an hour before the German forces entered the city!

Having brought the diamonds from Holland, it made good sense to have the location of the two brothers and their business as far away as possible from the British coastline, where raids and reprisals by enemy agents would be less likely or practical. For close protection the two brothers were provided with two bodyguards, who were given cover employment as part of the staff. The authors also wonder to what extent the Auxiliary patrols in Worcestershire were part of the protective screen around the two brothers.

Lewis, the elder of the two brothers, and Edmund or 'Gug' as he was known to the majority of the Auxiliers, after previously being based in London, lived at Ombersley until re-establishing their industrial diamond business at Lower Wolverton, near Peopleton. Here, at Wolverton Hall, the diamond processing was carried out in the the big house, employing local people on the production work. The location of the van Moppes' diamond processing business close to the war materials manufacturing industries in the West Midlands was also a factor in their coming to Worcestershire. After the war, the business was moved to new premises at Basingstoke and the van Moppes' connection with Worcestershire apparently severed. It is said that the diamonds spirited out of Holland in 1940 were returned, with interest, to their original owners after the war.

Of more direct interest to the story is the fact that the two brothers established the headquarters for the Auxiliary patrols in Worcestershire at Wolverton Hall. Here the patrol sergeants or other individuals from each of the patrols would report regularly for instructions. Patrol training exercises, and later competitions, to hone the Auxiliaries operational skills would also be undertaken here. Should a German invasion of Britain have occurred, a message carrying system, using relays of couriers, was organised to maintain contact between the patrols and their commanders, although currently we have little information on it. It is significant that a tunnel still exists at Wolverton Hall which leaves the cellars and leads into the garden. This would no doubt have been used to effect an escape had the house been surrounded by enemy forces.

The recruitment of the two brothers to the Auxiliaries was apparently a matter of chance. During 1940, Edmund met John Todd while playing bridge at Droitwich and expressed the view that he was dissatisfied with the role he

Wolverton Hall, the wartime home of the van Moppes brothers and headquarters of the Worcestershire Auxilairies. The group photographs shown elsewhere were taken on the terrace and steps in front of the door.
(Mick Wilks, courtesy of Susie Elliot)

was then playing in the Home Guard. Todd suggested that he had a job which might interest him and while he could not talk it about at the bridge party, suggested they meet one night at the Raven Hotel in Droitwich. This they did and John Todd drove Edmund around the area for half-an-hour while they discussed the role and before the latter was then asked to sign the Official Secrets Act at an office nearby. This office was almost certainly in the former Norbury Hotel which had been requisitioned by the army during the war. After finding out what the job entailed Edmund suggested that his brother would be interested too and so both were recruited to the Auxiliaries. The van Moopes were given the code names Castor and Pollux during their Auxiliary service although it is possible that these code names were the product of their earlier clandestine operation for MI6 to secure the Amsterdam diamonds.

Roger Smith, of Commandary Farm, Crowle was initially the Patrol Sergeant of the Auxilaries in that locality but was promoted in 1943 to the rank of Second Lieutenant and became the Group Leader for half of the Worcestershire patrols. These were Broadheath, Claines and Crowle patrols and were designated Group 1(b). At this stage Lewis van Moppes became a Captain and presumably the equivalent of an Intelligence Officer for Worcestershire. His brother, Edmund, became a full Lieutenant and Group Commander responsible for the Alfrick, Lenches and Overbury patrols.

To assist the van Moppes brothers and Roger Smith, a Quarter Master Sergeant was appointed. This was Sergeant Dawe, who apparently lived at Wolverton Hall and was also the van Moppes' Company Accountant.

CHAPTER 3
Disposition & perceived Strategy and Tactics

The map overleaf shows the disposition of known Auxiliary patrols in Herefordshire and Worcestershire. This was produced following assembly of the information on the individual patrols given in subsequent chapters. As far as the authors are aware, no documentary evidence has yet been traced of the tactical thinking behind the location of the inland patrols. However, analysed against the more conventional military defences put in place in the two counties and elsewhere in Britain to resist German invasion forces, this map does provide an insight into, and allow us to speculate upon, the strategy and tactics worked out by Captain Todd and his colleagues at Coleshill. No doubt too, John Todd would have been closely liaising with the military defence planners of Western Command at Chester.

Immediately obvious is the relationship of the majority of patrols to the wartime railway system. Destruction of sections of this system by the use of explosives would have had a seriously disruptive effect on the ability of German forces to move troops and supplies in support of further advances, particularly from the west and south. This strategy was to be successfully used later by SOE and the French Resistance to help disrupt the movement of German reinforcements and supplies to Normandy as a support to the invasion by allied forces on 6 June 1944, and the later allied advances into France.

Discernible too, are two lines of Auxiliary patrols: one closely related to the Wye valley; the other following part of the Teme valley and then forming an arc around Worcester. It is interesting to compare these with the more conventional military defences put in place both within and outside the two counties to resist enemy armoured thrusts from the south and west and from that comparison deduce the tactical thinking behind the location of the patrols. A brief description of the conventional defences is therefore included.

Essentially, the land-based anti-invasion strategy for the United Kingdom in the summer of 1940 was to defend all potential landing beaches and behind them create a series of defence lines, called stop-lines, and defended nodal points, should the enemy invasion forces have broken through the coastal

17

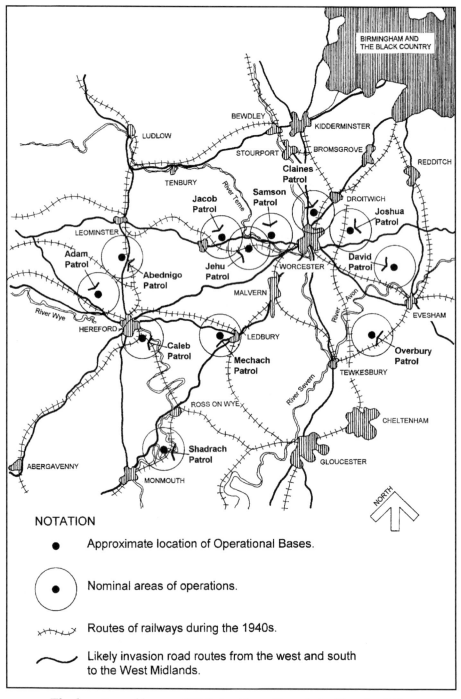

The location of known GHQ Auxiliary Patrols in Herefordshire and Worcestershire

defences. These inland defences were to prevent enemy armoured columns from having the relatively free movement that they had benefitted from during the successful German attacks on the Low Countries and France during May and June that year, and allow time for a counter-attack to be organised and directed. The expected main thrust of an invasion was correctly judged to be upon the south coast, but diversionary attacks on the east coast or the Welsh coast could also be expected and were planned for. Should the defenders on the coastal crust have failed to repel the German invasion forces, a second major line of defence was constructed inland and parallel to the south and east coasts, stretching from Bristol in the west towards London, then skirting the south and east sides of London before going northwards towards Scotland. This was known as the General Headquarters Line, or GHQ Line, behind which the main Regular Army reserve was to be stationed in order to form a counter-attack force, once the main thrust of the enemy had been established. A good survey of the extensive defences along the GHQ Line and the surviving archaeology is set out in *Ironside's Line* by Colin Alexander.

Behind the GHQ Line, the country was to be divided into 'fields' within which enemy columns would be trapped and dealt with by mobile columns of Regular troops. To hinder and enmesh the enemy armoured columns, which may have reached this far inland, a series of stop-lines were created to define the fields. Anti-tank islands were formed around the junctions of major roads or nodal points found within key towns and cities. The stop-lines and anti-tank islands were essentially static defences to be manned by the local Home Guard, leaving the responsibility for manoeuvre and counter-attack to the mobile columns of the Regular Army.

In the counties of Herefordshire and Worcestershire the rivers Avon, Severn, Teme and Wye were all designated in 1940 as stop lines. These natural water features were identified as ready-made anti-tank ditches which were fortuitously disposed to form protection for the main armaments industries of Birmingham, Coventry and the Black Country. The armaments industries were recognised by the home defence planners as being key objectives for the Germans, and enemy attacks from the west and/or south could be expected in order to capture them quickly and so limit our ability to fight back. They were therefore to be defended at all costs and to bolster the lines of defence, the main river crossings were provided with road blocks and various weapons positions, including trench systems, pillboxes and anti-tank artillery emplacements. It is significant that all the anti-tank artillery emplacements on the Severn Stop-Line were on the east side of the river and faced westwards. Should the defences at the river crossings have failed, then the bridges would have been destroyed with explosives previously placed in the bridge structures by Royal Engineer teams. The disruption of enemy supply lines through Herefordshire from the South Wales ports, and destruction of tank and vehicle laagers, fuel and ammu-

Above and left: One of the defences on the Severn Stop-Line—the Holt Fleet 6 pdr gun position. (Mick Wilks)

nition dumps, by the Auxiliaries in the Wye valley, operating behind the enemy columns, would have been an important element in the planned delaying tactics should an attack have been made from the west.

The towns of Redditch, Kidderminster and, most notably, the city of Worcester were all designated as anti-tank islands in 1940, and prepared for all round defence. At this early stage, none of the towns in Herefordshire were so designated, although by 1942 Hereford was included. The defences at Worcester were to be extensive and included several concentric lines of defence, comprising barbed wire entanglements, anti-tank ditches, numerous road blocks, pillboxes, fortified and loopholed buildings, artillery and sub-artillery emplacements (as the Home Guard called them), slit trenches, machinegun posts and even an armoured train. Minefields were also proposed. The purpose behind all these defences, many of which were actually completed, was to deny the German forces for as long as possible the use of the many main roads through Worcestershire that converged in the centre of Worcester, as well as the main river crossing there.

The widespread works, both nationally and locally and briefly described above, were quickly constructed during the summer of 1940 and into 1941 and were the greatest military engineering feat Britain had known. Most local authorities, civil engineering companies, house builders and of course the Royal Engineers were involved in this massive undertaking.

Little now remains locally of those extensive defences, but it is possible to imagine a siege being mounted by the Germans surrounding Worcester, where the Home Guard defenders had been instructed to hold their positions 'to the last round and the last man'. Anyone who remembers the post-war traffic jams in Worcester, before the M5 Motorway was built, and with only one river crossing, will know that the Germans would have been hard put to get through Worcester, even without the attention of the Home Guard defenders! The Broadheath, Claines and Crowle Auxiliary patrols were well placed to disrupt the assembly of tanks and other armoured vehicles for such an attack, while the patrols further away would have would been able to sabotage the troop convoys and aircraft bringing enemy reinforcements towards the city. It is significant that three Auxiliary patrols were concentrated along the A44 from Bromyard to Worcester, where it passes through the Knightwick gap in the north-south range of hills which divide the two counties. It is very likely therefore that the Auxiliary patrols in Worcestershire were part of the carefully worked out plans for defending the city, particularly against an attack from the west.

The Knightwick Gap—the likely route of German invasion forces from South Wales heading towards the industrial heartlands. The wartime road and the old bridge site over the Teme are to the left. (Mick Wilks)

How the Home Guard urban saboteurs discussed in chapter 10 were to fit into the plan for defending the city is not yet clear, especially since critics of such a role for the Home Guard felt that they would have confused the more conventional arm of the force. Perhaps their time would have come after the city had been occupied, when their role would have been to tie down as many of the German troops as possible by acts of sabotage and so prevent their participation in enemy attacks against Birmingham, Coventry and the Black Country.

This brief description of the conventional military defences and the relationship of the Auxiliary patrols in Herefordshire and Worcestershire to them provides compelling evidence of the importance given by the 1940s defence planners to the protection of the vital armaments industries of Birmingham, Coventry and the Black Country from an enemy attack from the west, either through South Wales, or from the Bristol Channel and up the Severn Valley. It is significant too that the Auxiliary Units in Herefordshire and Worcestershire were the furthest inland. Elsewhere in Britain, the Auxiliary patrols were just inland from the south coasts of both England and Wales, and the east coast from Kent as far north as Scotland. In the autumn of 1940 or the spring of 1941, the preliminary and critical battles for the West Midlands manufacturing base could well have been fought in the two counties with these inland Auxiliaries providing an important, and perhaps even decisive, element of the defences.

CHAPTER 4
Coleshill House

Unlike other county Units, which were trained by local Army Scout Patrols, the main intensive training for the Worcestershire and Herefordshire patrols was carried out at Coleshill House near Swindon in Wiltshire. The house had been built in the 17th century by the architect Sir Roger Platt, and was owned by the Pleydell-Bouverie family; other houses owned by the family in the New Forest would be used by SOE for the training of agents. In 1940 Coleshill House became the headquarters of the Auxiliary Units, sealed against prying eyes by a high brick wall and with spacious grounds for intensive training.

After the departure of Gubbins to SOE in late 1940, Lt-Colonel Major was appointed his successor with Major Beyts remaining in place as the other principal officer. Major's office was situated in the library of the house, and his secretary was an ATS sergeant, 'Willie' Willmott. For two years Beyts was to play a crucial role in organising the training and fashioning the identity and enthusiasm of the Units. In February 1942 Colonel The Lord Glanusk took over responsibility at Coleshill from Major. Just over a year later, Colonel Douglas RA, who would be the last commander of the Units, took his place.

Officers were accommodated in the house although other ranks slept in outbuildings. Whilst visiting Auxiliers might have to rough it, the officers did enjoy a little more comfort. The wealthy Major Beddington-Behrens, a friend of Gubbins, brought his horse to the house, and slept in satin sheets. Meals were eaten in a common room and all ranks messed together.

Weekend courses were held in the use of explosives, unarmed combat, silent killing, and weapon and grenade skills, map reading and field craft. A detachment of Lovat Scouts demonstrated the techniques of stalking and field craft whilst Royal Engineer officers trained the Auxiliers in the use of explosives and detonators. Unarmed combat ('thuggery') was demonstrated by members of the Army School of Physical Training, with detailed instruction given to enable the Auxilier to respond with confidence to various situations. One example, giving the flavour of 'thuggery' and obtained from written instructions given at Coleshill, is as follows:

Coleshill House, Highworth, Wiltshire, from an 18th-century engraving.
(Mick Wilks Collection)

Releases and throws when attacked from behind:

If held around the waist from behind, you can make your opponent release you immediately by-:

a) Grasping his head or clothing and throwing him over your head.

b) Or stoop quickly forward, seize one of his legs as near the ankle as possible. Pull it vigorously upward, at the same time throwing all your weight backward. This would result in your opponent falling very heavily, with you landing on his middle and winding him completely. Once your opponent is at your mercy, a leg, arm or strangle hold can be applied.

At least one model Operational Base for Auxiliary Units was built in the park for training purposes, for one still remains.

Once the patrols were adequately trained, they would later return to Coleshill to enter into inter-patrol competitions. Efficiency with explosives was an obvious test and the men would be set the task of making up charges to deal with a range of tasks, such as tree cutting and the setting alight of a petrol dump. A number of tests were given to cover the use of booby traps, and knowledge of fuses and time pencils. The ability to move around the countryside was tested by map reading exercises including the giving of accurate map references. Skill at arms involved the firing of the Sten gun and revolver and the accurate throwing of a grenade. More complex problems and night exercises were set for participants in the Coleshill Shield Competition.

Existing outbuildings at Coleshill House were used as offices by HQ staff or as living accommodation for Auxiliers undergoing training. (Bernard Lowry)

When Auxiliers arrived to report at Coleshill they often had to go through a 'reception' procedure at the local post office in Highworth. The memories of Geoff Devereux, the initial Patrol Sergeant of Samson Patrol in Worcestershire are particularly useful because they dispel a myth that exaggerates the role of the then Post Mistress, Mrs Mabel Stranks, which implied that she personally vetted all Auxiliary recruits presenting themselves at the post office. Nevertheless the procedure is intriguing and her role was important. Geoff was told to go into the post office and ask for five three-ha'penny stamps and to hand over a half-crown coin; John Todd, the Intelligence Officer overseeing the patrol, had specifically checked that Geoff had a half-crown coin before he was dropped off. This precise order and use of the half-crown was the signal for Mrs Stranks to go into the back of the post office to telephone Coleshill and tell them that: 'One of your lot is here. Could you pick him up?'. The combination of Geoff being dressed in denims and the specific order for the stamps was the only introduction to the system. There was no handing over of any 'chitty', which would normally be expected, and there was certainly no vetting by Mrs Stranks. As Geoff says: 'all the vetting had already been carried out by John Todd'.

Basil Tadman of the Overbury Patrol says that initial training for the whole patrol was undertaken at Coleshill and can remember going to the post office in Highworth, from where they were picked up and taken to the HQ. Here they were trained in the use of explosives, night patrolling and grenade throwing into a steel container. The grenade throwing was by the conventional over-arm method, rather than the side throw as might be employed by a cricket fielder, which we understand some Auxiliaries used as a more accurate way of getting the grenades into the target container. Perhaps this method was used only for competitions?

The former post office, Highworth, near Swindon. It was to here that all written communications were sent, the address also serving as the cover for Coleshill House—'c/o G.P.O. Highworth', and where Auxiliers, at least in the earlier years of the war, would 'report' when arriving for training.
(Bernard Lowry)

Several members of the Herefordshire and Worcestershire patrols, including Horace Phillips and Bill Plaskett of Jehu Patrol, have no recollection of going through the post office routine. As their visit was in the winter of 1941/42 perhaps this introduction to Coleshill had been abandoned by then; once the initial threat of invasion was over it may have been felt that this procedure was unnecessary.

At Coleshill, Horace and Bill Plaskett received training in the use of grenades, including the Sticky Bomb, and how to blow up a tank hidden in the woods. The first task was to find the tank, which itself proved difficult. The pair were supplied with their Smith and Wesson revolvers here and received training and practise in their use. Horace does not recall having the Fairbairn-Sykes knife but says they were given instruction in unarmed combat.

Jim Griffin, who joined Jehu Patrol in early 1942, spent three days at Coleshill and can recall that his instructor for unarmed combat and grenade training was Lieutenant Patterson. During the grenade training he was told that if he dropped a live one in the trench then he would have to deal with it himself—this was just after a British sergeant elsewhere had thrown himself onto a grenade, which had been dropped inside a practise trench, in order to

26

save the other members of the grenade party, and had been killed. This was thought by Patterson to be an incredibly brave thing to do but if the same thing happened at Coleshill, then he would leave the trainees to it! The training included how to immobilise a sentry who would be turned on to his stomach with his hands and feet tied up together so that he was unable to move, other

A photograph taken on 5 February 1941 of Intelligence Officers and Headquarters staff at Coleshill House. The variety of uniforms is noteworthy.
Left to right:
Back Row: Major The Lord Ashley, Captain Ian Fenwick, Captain Bond.
Third Row: Captain K.W. Johnson, Captain John Todd, Captain Gwynne, Captain Darwell-Smith(?), Captain E.B. Clive, Captain Field.
Second Row: Captain J.W. Edmundson, Captain G.C.L. Atkinson, Captain Hamilton-Hill, Major Beddington-Behrens, Captain E. Maxwell, Captain W.E. Clark.
Front Row: Captain Torrence, Captain N.V. Oxenden MC, Lt.-Colonel G.H.B. 'Billy' Beyts MC, Colonel C.R. Major, Major The Hon. M.T. Henderson, Captain W.W. Harston, Captain Crosthwaite-Eyre, Lieutenant Anderson.

Colonel Major was the Commanding Officer of the Auxiliary Units at this time, with Lt-Colonel Beyts the Second-in-Command; Captain John Todd was the Intelligence Officer for Units in Monmouthshire, Herefordshire and Worcestershire from July 1940 until 1942; Captain K.W. Johnson fulfilled the same role for Units in Glamorgan until 1943 when he took over Intelligence Officer Special Duties role for Herefordshire and Worcestershire from Captain Bucknall. (Courtesy of Miss E.M. Wilmot)

A later photograph, showing the growth in the number of Intelligence and Headquarters' officers, taken at Coleshill House on 28 January 1942. Captain Todd had left the Auxiliary Units to join SOE and his replacement, Captain Sandford, stands at the rear in front of the house doors and wearing a Field Service Cap. To the left of him, wearing a peaked cap, is Anthony Quayle. Colonels Major and Beyts are still in charge and two ATS Special Duties officers, Barbara Culleton and Beatrice Temple, join the men in the photograph. On the right of Colonel Major is Major Petherick MP, who was in charge of the Special Duties Section. (Mick Wilks collection)

than to rock back and forth. This method of dealing with enemy sentries contrasts markedly with the more bloodthirsty exhortations of Captain Todd in the early days of the Auxiliaries.

Another memory Jim has of his time at Coleshill is of sitting next to the then Commanding Officer of the Auxiliaries, Lord Glanusk, at mealtimes. Apparently no-one else wanted to sit by the CO but Jim found him to be very easy to get on with. This departure from the normal military protocol, with officers and the recruits taking meals together, is perhaps an indication of the respect the Auxiliary Units Headquarters staff had for these civilian volunteers.

Throughout the life of the Auxiliary Units, Coleshill House provided a secure headquarters and training facility. The range of subjects covered is testimony to the high standards of skill and intelligence required of the Units' members.

Coleshill remained in use until the Units were stood down in late 1944. Sadly, the house was destroyed in a fire in September 1952.

CHAPTER 5
Operational Bases

Soon after the establishment of the Headquarters staff of the GHQ Auxiliary Units, it was decided that the civilians being recruited to the Auxiliary patrols should have hidden bases from which to carry out their clandestine operations, store their arms and explosives and live for an indeterminate time. These hideouts were to be heavily camouflaged and conveniently sited within the area of operations. Most of the bases in the counties of Herefordshire and Worcestershire were underground structures, normally built by squads of Royal Engineers and Pioneers. These troops were brought into the area from other parts of the UK in order that they would not know the area and so be a security risk. However, this was not always the case and in some cases local builders or estate workers were used to build the bases, sworn to secrecy of course. In one instance an existing above ground building was adapted, while another of the patrols made use of caves.

Very soon after the first 'hideouts' for the Auxiliaries were provided, it was decided by Colonel Gubbins and his staff that such a descriptive term was too obvious and posed a security risk. The new term chosen to refer to the structures from then onwards would be Operational Base or OB, this innocuous combination of words or letters being thought to be a better disguise for the form or possible location of the bases.

In all cases in the two counties the OBs were located on private land. The then owners must therefore have been 'in the know' and sworn to secrecy. It is significant that a number of the landowners were either retired army officers, who could be trusted to keep the knowledge of the OB secret, or were themselves Auxiliers. Most of the OBs were demolished at the end of the war by the Regular Army, usually Royal Engineers personnel, preventing possible use by undesirable characters. Demolition was often carried out using the Auxiliers' own explosives and ammunition. However, because of the secrecy surrounding their location and the fact that there were no written records kept, a few OBs were missed in this procedure and are now a focus for the curious. The authors have visited a number of OB sites and where these structures still exist, or there are obvious signs of their former presence, such as a large hollow, all the landowners in the two counties have, without exception, made it clear that casual visitors to the sites are not welcome. Those structures which still exist are now 60 years old, and dangerous. References to the location of OBs have, therefore, been kept deliberately vague to discourage casual visits to the sites.

One of the first Operational Bases to be constructed in the two counties was that for Samson Patrol, near Broadwas. Before it was constructed, Geoff Devereux, the patrol sergeant, was very dubious about using an OB as a base for their operations and could envisage the patrol being trapped there by enemy troops. Having carefully chosen the site of the base and seen how professionally it was constructed and camouflaged, he changed his opinion about it. This OB no longer exists so there are only the memories of the surviving members of the patrol to tell us of its form. Fortunately Geoff Devereux has given us a most comprehensive description of his OB.

> The OB was in the shape of a Nissen hut, approximately 12 feet below ground level. There was a vertical shaft as the main entrance, about 2 feet square, with a tree stump set in a concrete lid and some sort of counter-weight to enable it to be opened from the outside or the inside. There were also two escape/access tunnels, about 3 feet square and lined with timber and corrugated iron. All entrances were beautifully camouflaged. I can remember that, when John Todd showed me the design of the OB, I was concerned about the short escape tunnel that was to be provided and I told him it was quite inadequate! I wanted two tunnels, one each side of the ridgeline, so that we had a choice of escape if the main entrance was discovered. One of the tunnels was finally about 70 feet long when completed. I also told him that I wanted a sump at the bottom of the entrance shaft so that if a grenade was thrown in, it would explode beneath the level of the entrance door of the OB.
>
> The main chamber of the OB was divided into three sections. The living section had some camp chairs, a paraffin camp cooker, pressure light, camp table and shelves, wash basin and chemical toilet. In the sleeping section were four two tier bunks and the store section was subdivided into food store and arsenal. We had sufficient provisions for a month and a water tank. One surprising item of stores was a gallon cask of Army rum labelled with a very strict warning of penalties if used before an invasion.
>
> We were very fortunate in our village, we had a very good Boy Scout troop, with a wonderful Scout Master, who insisted on the very highest standards of scouting. Most of the members of our unit were from the village scout troop, all well trained and experienced campers, so that our OB was really a touch of comfort compared with the tents of those days. We could all cook and our field craft was of a high order. We were well known to each other and got along well. As village boys we came from

homes without electricity and running water so the lack of these facilities was no hardship and we enjoyed sleeping in our OB.

The sump provided at the bottom of the entrance shaft of the Samson Patrol OB was two or three feet deeper than the general floor level. This appears to have been a unique feature in OB design—surprisingly such a logical idea was not adopted elsewhere. The construction of two escape tunnels also appears to be unique and the camouflaged exits into thick bushes allowed the patrol to have unobtrusive surveillance of the surrounding area. This provision for escape contrasts markedly with OBs elsewhere in the two counties which could well have been death traps for the occupants. Geoff continues:

Two stores were provided, one for food and the other for explosives and arms. Near the food store, or larder, was a cooking area with a paraffin cooker and the necessary utensils, Tilley lamps, water tank, etc. There was enough tinned food for at least a month and it was planned to replenish the water from the River Teme, a few hundred yards away. In addition to the tins of food and the gallon of rum, we also had our own supply of bottled beer and lemonade. We had snares in our OB for rabbits and pheasants and we had recce'd a cottage bakery on Broadheath Common, where bread was baked each day for sale the next day. We intended to relieve the baker of some loaves (and leave the money) after he had retired for the night! With our snares and the silenced .22 rifle we could have survived for food for a long period, having also noted local fields planted with potatoes, swedes, etc. We also had bank lines to set in the Teme nearby, for eels and trout, and we actually did poach fish and game to prove a point. We had a big stew pot and we would put all the ingredients in the pot to cook. There was a fold down table for eating and preparation of explosive charges, six folding chairs and a board on which we pinned various instruction sheets. Ammunition and explosives were kept in metal boxes and detonators in a separate cupboard. We also built carefully sited caches for the 'nasties', i.e. Phosphorous Grenades, Sticky Bombs etc. near the OB and well camouflaged. The arms in the OB consisted of Thompson sub-machinegun, revolvers, automatic pistols and plenty of ammunition. We also had plastic explosive (I think about 100 lbs). I remember John Todd telling me, when he delivered it, that it was sufficient to demolish Worcester Bridge over the Severn if properly applied, but for our purposes, it should disable or destroy 100 tanks. In addition we had a lot of time-delay pencils, booby trap switches, delayed action and instantaneous safety fuse, detonating cord, detonators, hand grenades, Sticky Bombs and of course our Commando daggers.

The excellent provision of the OB and the contents made us feel very professional and competent, and we felt we had the tools for the job, especially when we saw the local Home Guards and their ancient shotguns and rifles from WWI. We were actually better armed than the

Regular Army at the time. I can remember John Todd telling me that Winston Churchill had insisted on this.

The OB was apparently built very quickly by a platoon of 'sappers' and Pioneers who were brought down from Scotland, specifically so that they would have no local knowledge or contacts. They had been briefed to tell any

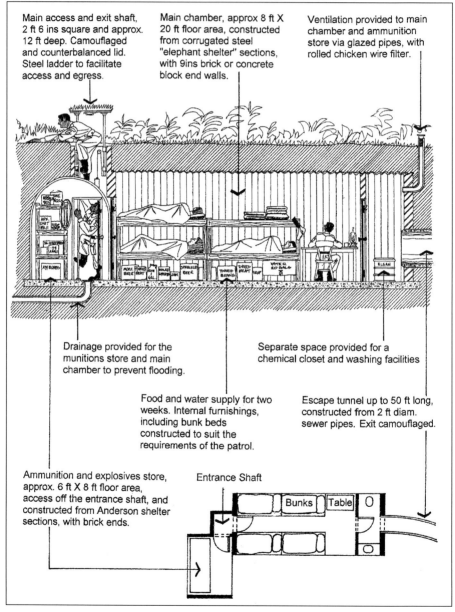

Section through a typical Auxiliary patrol Operational Base in Worcestershire

inquisitive locals that they were examining possible sites for Ack-Ack guns. This was a common cover story used by Royal Engineer squads constructing OBs elsewhere to put off curious locals intent on finding out what was going on. The authors have spoken to a number of people who recall that the Royal Engineers were spotted bringing materials to other OB sites in the two counties, notably at Alfrick and at Crowle. It is just as well that there was not an invasion by the Germans because the curiosity of these people would have almost certainly have meant the security of the patrols would have been compromised. This must have been a constant worry to the Auxiliaries and it is likely that, because they posed a security risk, such people would have been added to their list of unfortunates to be assassinated.

At Crowle the first OB was built in a woodland, then owned by the Croome Estate, where, surprisingly, people were allowed to continue shooting game with the inevitable result that the presence of this OB was spotted, although its purpose was not apparently guessed. One person who remembers seeing the site was Jim Colebrooke who, when out shooting, came across an area of obviously disturbed ground which had been replanted with the indigenous hazelnut bushes. These had not taken and were dying back. He had also seen the Royal Engineer construction party entering the wood and guessed that the structure had some military significance but did not investigate it further. It was only recently when helping with our enquiries that he was made aware of its true purpose! A number of local people had also seen these same Royal Engineers travelling in lorries from Norton Barracks, where they had been billeted, and bringing the construction materials to Crowle. This OB was obviously badly compromised and it is perhaps fortunate that it was abandoned and replaced by another, as described later. Inevitably, too, a number of OBs were discovered by children, and in one case Boy Scouts, who were exploring the woods in the county, during wartime or afterwards.

While Geoff Devereux's OB appears to have been one of the more sophisticated structures, it bears a strong similarity to other structures described by Auxiliaries elsewhere as being like a small, underground Nissen hut. In fact this structure was called an 'elephant shelter' by the staff at Coleshill. Although of the same curved form of the Nissen hut, it was smaller in cross section, had larger corrugations, and was formed from thicker material in order to better withstand the weight and pressure from the earth overburden. The structure provided about 8 feet of headroom at the apex and was about 10 feet in width. The length of the OBs could be varied and in some cases, like Geoff Devereux's, was subdivided to form storage and ablutions facilities.

The best surviving example of an OB seen by the authors is the one constructed for the Alfrick Patrol and, while some of the structure has now collapsed, it is possible to see that the munitions store was a separate structure connected to, and to one side of, the access shaft and formed from Anderson shelter sections. This surviving structure has provided enough detail to produce the drawing on p..32 of a typical OB in use.

After digging, by hand, the large hole necessary to accommodate the OB—machinery would have been too obvious—the construction party would re-cover the completed structure with some of the excavated top-soil and replant indigenous woodland trees and shrubs over the area to disguise its presence. From the Samson Patrol OB access to the River Teme was quite good and Geoff Devereux thought that a lot of the excavated soil was tipped into the river near the oxbow lake. The bushes and small trees here also survived well when trans-planted because there was plenty of water available from the river. In fact when John Todd first took him to his OB Geoff was surprised how well the camou-flage had grown in such a short time. The OB was impossible to see and this did much to reduce his earlier misgivings. With other OBs the residue of top and sub-soil appears to have been spread about in the close vicinity to minimise carrying it and limit disturbance in the woodland. This too was replanted to help speed the camouflage. However, despite these efforts by the Engineers to disguise their activities, even now it is possible in some cases to spot the unnat-ural spread of the spoil nearby! Dick Philips recalls that his patrol improved the camouflage of their OB by spreading over it the plentiful fallen leaves, which also supplied a means to cover their tracks when they were using it.

From investigating the OB sites in the two counties, there appears to have been a fairly consistent approach to the siting of the structures. Whether this was as a result of GHQ policy or the influence of Captain Todd is not clear, but all were located in woodland or small copses to provide some cover from the prying eyes of Luftwaffe reconnaissance aircraft or the foot patrols of enemy occupation troops. The ground chosen was inevitably sloping and the OB would normally be constructed near the top of the slope to take advantage of the drier subsoil conditions and to permit easier drainage of the structure. A location near an existing woodland ride or well-used footpath was also invari-ably chosen to reduce the amount of disturbance to the surrounding under-growth by the patrol going to and from the OB. A nearby supply of fresh water, usually a stream, was also a feature.

Access to the OBs was normally via a vertical brick-built shaft. A series of steel rungs would be provided for the Auxiliaries to climb in and out and from those which still exist, it is possible to see that the shafts were actually about 2 foot 6 inches square. None of the lids survive but most have been described as being of wooden construction with a tray of soil on them which was planted with grass and small woodland shrubs, or as having been covered with bitumi-nous felt and chicken wire into which were placed branches or other plant material to provide camouflage. The most sophisticated form of cover was as described by Geoff Devereux and included a part of a tree stump in its disguise. While some covers were simply hinged, the heavier forms of disguise would require a more complex counterbalanced lifting device. The tree trunk form of camouflage for the entrance is also known to have been used by the Overbury patrol.

John Boaz, who joined Samson Patrol in July 1941, recalls being taken to their OB for the first time. This was alongside one of the woodland rides so that a separate path to it was avoided. He was then asked if he could see anything but, although recently constructed, it was so well camouflaged with shrubs and small trees that he could not! He was shown how to enter the OB. This involved putting a hand into a rabbit hole under the stump of an old tree, pulling a lever which moved a further piece of wood, which in turn allowed the stump to be moved, revealing the entrance shaft. This had a chamfered edge into which the tree stump dropped, with sufficient overlap so that when in position, nothing of the lid could be seen.

Roy Robinson, of Mechach Patrol, thought the entry into their Operational Base was quite ingenious. The lid, camouflaged by vegetation, was a round one raised by a spindle and crank handle. Inside, an anteroom held an Elsan toilet, tinned food and explosives. In the main chamber were bunks. The entire bunker may have been built of concrete: the floor was certainly of concrete. A three feet diameter concrete pipe provided an emergency exit and led to a point twelve feet away, where there was an opening under a yew tree.

Jehu Patrol's OB still exists, although the main chamber has partially collapsed and the structure is now in a dangerous condition. It is the fairly standard corrugated metal 'elephant shelter' structure with vertical shaft entrance and sewer pipe escape tunnel. A munitions store is provided to one side of the vertical shaft and this is constructed with Anderson shelter sections. The entrance was camouflaged with a wooden, hinged lid that had bituminous felt covering with chicken wire, into which foliage would be fixed. Leaves, scattered round the lid, were used to complete the camouflage once it had been closed. The lid has now gone.

Dampness inside these OBs was a continual problem. Samson patrol's John Boaz relates that despite being finished internally with a cork-based composition to provide some insulation, their OB was very damp. In order to improve the ventilation, the OB was provided later with a system of glazed drainpipes to encourage a flow of air. This required much nocturnal digging by the members of the patrol, whilst the pipes themselves were 'borrowed' from the council who were doing some drainage work at Kenswick.

Dampness particularly affected those OBs built with corrugated metal and as a result most patrols moved their arms, ammunition and explosives to drier, secure, accommodation elsewhere. On receiving a code message indicating an enemy invasion was occurring, the patrols would have quickly moved their equipment back to the OB, ready for action. A more effective method of dealing with the problem of dampness would have been the use of dehumidifiers, and indeed the HQ staff at Coleshill did order paraffin fired devices which had been developed by the RAF for preventing condensation in stored aircraft. How widely these were issued to the Auxiliary patrols is not clear and certainly none are remembered by the surviving Auxiliers as being issued to those in the counties of Herefordshire and Worcestershire.

All the patrols in the two counties spent weekends and sometimes longer occupying their OBs in order to practise the routines of living underground, carrying out night patrols, and of course catering for themselves. Lighting in the OBs was provided by either a Tilly lamp—a paraffin fired, pressure operated lamp—which gives out a very powerful light, or simply candles that provided a much softer light which was less likely to damage the Auxiliaries' night vision. Cooking was undertaken normally on a primus stove, again a paraffin, pressure operated device. Paraffin heaters were used to improve the comfort of the OBs and the use of this liquid for cooking, lighting as well as heating must have exacerbated the problem of condensation because it is now recognised, if not then, that the burning of paraffin creates many times its own weight in water. This, together with the problems of inadequate ventilation, must have made living underground for any length of time uncomfortable to say the least.

Some of the patrols in the two counties provided Observation Posts for themselves. These were sited some distance from the OB but normally connected to it by the standard Army Field Telephone. The OP would provide space for one patrol member to scan the locality for enemy troop movements, potential targets or any threat to the patrol's safety. In one case a nearby tower was used for this purpose but two special OP sites which have been positively identified were located under the dark and overhanging branches of yew trees where the observer would be well hidden in their dugouts, even in winter.

The signal for the Auxiliary patrol members to leave their families and occupy their OB in the event of an invasion would have been received in the form of a telephoned message to the Sergeant from the Group Leader. The message was simply: 'The Balloon has gone up'. We shall never know what reasons the patrol members would have given to their families for disappearing totally. Jim Holt, of Joshua Patrol, recalled that it was a constant difficulty for him to make up excuses to his wife when he went off for a weekend's training or a practise occupation of the OB, without telling her what he was actually up to. Many of the married Auxiliaries were, no doubt, accused of 'seeing someone else' by their wives! What the men would have said if they had been called for active service, when they had no idea when, or if, they would return is difficult to imagine. How the message would have passed to one another and how they would have assembled is not known, although it is likely to have been based on the snowball system the conventional Home Guard used when an emergency was called. Here the geographical spread of the people would have dictated the routine but basically the Sergeant would tell the next nearest to him, this person would tell the next nearest to him and so on until all were aware of the emergency, each one leaving for the assembly point after passing on the message. It can be imagined that the Auxiliaries would have waited until darkness had fallen before assembling at their OB, each taking a different and well-practised route to reach it. This was to avoid suspicion and the possibility of giving away the position to any possible fifth columnists, who would also have been alerted to the invasion having occurred.

Once assembled the routine would have followed that developed from their training weekends. On these the men would have a supper before sleeping until morning, but not before helping themselves to a tot of rum from the gallon cask supplied for emergencies. After breakfast a scout or scouts left the OB at about 10 a.m. The scouts would normally be wearing civilian clothes for this role; Samson Patrol's technique, described by Geoff Devereux, was to dress in overalls and cycle around their operational area. Operational areas were nominally 20 square miles in extent for each patrol, and a number of Auxiliers remembering practising night patrols of 4 or 5 miles out and back to their OBs would tend to confirm this. The scouts would return to the OB at about 5 p.m. and report on what they had seen and their ideas for potential sabotage targets. Meanwhile the remainder of the patrol would have spent the day resting. The evening would then be spent with the Sergeant working out their plans for that night's attack, while the rest of the patrol would be busy making up the explosive charges ready for use and cleaning their weapons. After dark, the patrol, initially led by the Sergeant, would leave the OB at a slow walking pace in single file and at intervals to avoid bunching. The spacing between each would be about five paces to reduce the casualties caused by any booby trap encountered or the chances of being spotted by enemy patrols. The scouts would be left behind to rest, their work having been done. The explosive charges prepared earlier would be spread amongst the patrol, carrying them strapped around their middle, with grenades and ammunition stuffed in their pockets. On their journey, the patrol would stop at intervals to ensure that no one became lost in the darkness and would restart their march with someone else leading to share the responsibility. On reaching the vicinity of the target area the patrol would split up to reconnoitre the target using different routes. The reconnaissance would be carried out by crawling and would include testing for trip wires with a piece of grass held up in front of them. With this they could feel for a trip wire without setting it off. Anyone finding a trip would deactivate it before proceeding.

After the reconnaissance the patrol would reassemble at a pre-arranged place and time, when the Sergeant would decide which was the best means of approaching the target. All members of the patrol would start their time pencils together, re-enter the target area and place their charges for best effect. By 3 a.m. the patrol would leave the target area having used time pencils of appropriate delay to allow them to regain their OB before the charges exploded. The return journey to their OB would be made as cautiously as their departure. After eating, the patrol would retire to bed. The next day a different scout or scouts would do the reconnaissance work, so that this aspect of their work would be shared, and the procedure for an attack on a different target repeated the following night.

Not all the patrols chose to use their OBs operationally. Alex Beck, the Sergeant leading Adam Patrol in Herefordshire, decided that each member of his patrol should retain a complete set of equipment locally. If called to action, the patrol members, after an initial planning meeting, would go off to carry out individual acts of sabotage. His view was that his patrol would be more effective operating as individuals than tied to an operational base.

Patrols would not normally seek confrontation with the enemy but go about their work as silently and unobtrusively as possible. Occasionally an ambush might be deliberately planned, in which case a single vehicle, such as a staff car, or perhaps a despatch rider would be attacked. The issue of phosphorous AW Bombs and No. 74 Sticky Bombs to the Auxiliaries in the early stages of their existence, and normally used in a confrontational action with tanks, were provided for this purpose. However the Auxiliaries were not trained as infantrymen and would be at a disadvantage in a firefight. Nevertheless they were trained to kill sentries silently, should they be discovered while about their normal clandestine work. Their revolver, grenades or the automatic weapon were to be used for protection only, where they might have to fight their way out of difficulty. In the summer of 1941, the incendiary anti-tank devices were withdrawn which suggests that someone in authority had decided that ambushes were perhaps not the right form of action for Auxiliaries, the risk of death or injury being much higher. The AW Bombs were in any case proving to be difficult to store adequately and many were buried or destroyed when they deteriorated, for there was a real possibility of self-ignition.

For the assassination function of the Auxiliaries, one member of the patrol would be chosen as a sniper, usually the best shot, and his role would be to pick off enemy sentries or officers. Geoff Devereux remembers that he was given an envelope by John Todd and instructed to open this only when the invasion occurred. He does not know what was in it but may well have contained a hit list of collaborators for the patrol to deal with; we will probably never know. The .22 silenced rifle, fitted with a telescopic sight, was issued for this purpose but its efficiency in this role was doubted by many of the Auxiliaries: the long bullet needed to achieve the requisite power is certainly not silent in flight and the short bullet with the lower velocity and relative silence is not up to the job. However, its usefulness in dealing with tracker dogs or poaching game for food is not doubted. Some of the Auxiliaries remember having the .300 P17 rifle in their armoury, which was powerful, accurate, and more appropriate for sniping, but far from silent.

CHAPTER 6
Equipment and Weapons

Uniform

The appearance of the Auxilier in uniform was very similar to that of the Home Guard volunteer, with one or two exceptions. The most obvious difference lay in the display on the battle dress blouse sleeve of the relevant Auxiliary Units Battalion numbers: 201, 202 or 203.

For operations where absolute silence was required, rubber waterproof ankle boots or Plimsolls replaced ankle boots. Headgear would consist of the Field Service Cap on which was pinned the badge of the county regiment, although in training or on operations it is believed that Balaclavas would often have been worn. Whilst not standard issue, commercially available knitting patterns encouraged the production of Balaclavas, gloves and scarves by wives, mothers or girlfriends. For further camouflage the Auxilier would use burnt cork or mud on his face and hands to reduce his visibility at night.

The large webbing ammunition pouches worn by the Home Guard do not appear to have been supplied to the Auxiliary Units. Ammunition, explosives, and grenades would have been carried on the person or in a sandbag.

Weapons

As with the Home Guard, the majority of weapons used by the Units originated in the United States. In July 1940 President Roosevelt's envoy, William 'Wild Bill' Donovan, visited Britain to assess the island's chances of survival. The US Ambassador, Joseph Kennedy, had given a pessimistic forecast to Roosevelt and a second opinion was sought. Amongst other displays, a demonstration by Gubbins' Auxiliary Units in East Anglia impressed Donovan and a favourable report was sent back to Washington. Roosevelt agreed to supply weapons to Britain forthwith, and the newly formed Home Guard and Auxiliary Units would have the weapons they needed that month. Donovan would later head the Office of Strategic Service, the equivalent of our SOE and SIS (MI6) and would have contact with Gubbins at SOE throughout the war, although the relationship between the two organisations would not always be harmonious.

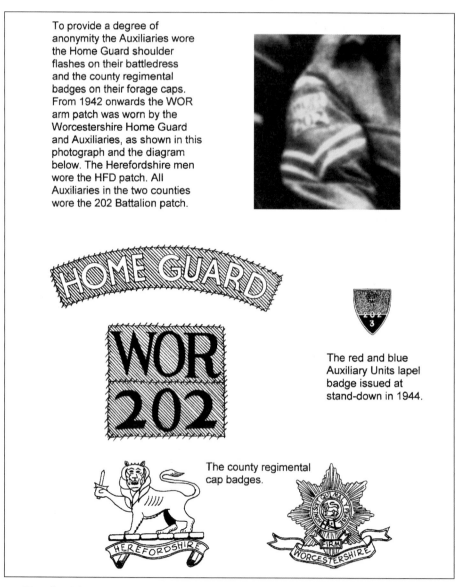

To provide a degree of anonymity the Auxiliaries wore the Home Guard shoulder flashes on their battledress and the county regimental badges on their forage caps. From 1942 onwards the WOR arm patch was worn by the Worcestershire Home Guard and Auxiliaries, as shown in this photograph and the diagram below. The Herefordshire men wore the HFD patch. All Auxiliaries in the two counties wore the 202 Battalion patch.

The red and blue Auxiliary Units lapel badge issued at stand-down in 1944.

The county regimental cap badges.

Herefordshire and Worcestershire Auxiliary Patrols Insignia and Badges

The types of weapon supplied to the patrols reflected the operational role of the Units. This was not to get engaged in a pitched battle, but to carry out sabotage or attack missions as quietly and as quickly as possible and to withdraw. For this reason they were not provided with heavy weapons. However, they were given weapons for close defence or the elimination of sentries. For the latter role, the primary weapon was the Fairbairn-Sykes dagger, also supplied to élite units of the Army, designed by Captains Fairbairn and Sykes. Both men

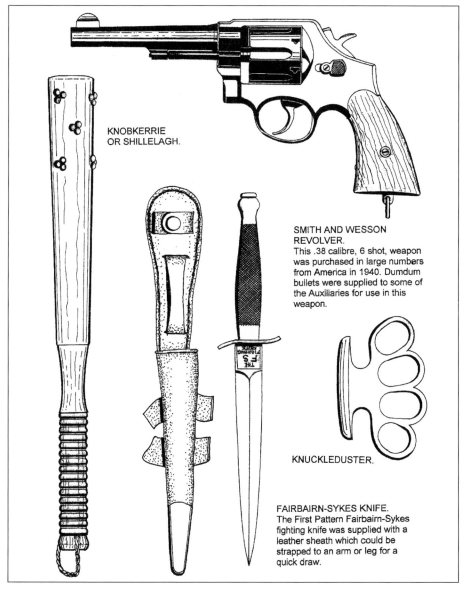

KNOBKERRIE
OR SHILLELAGH.

SMITH AND WESSON
REVOLVER.
This .38 calibre, 6 shot, weapon
was purchased in large numbers
from America in 1940. Dumdum
bullets were supplied to some of
the Auxiliaries for use in this
weapon.

KNUCKLEDUSTER.

FAIRBAIRN-SYKES KNIFE.
The First Pattern Fairbairn-Sykes
fighting knife was supplied with a
leather sheath which could be
strapped to an arm or leg for a
quick draw.

Personal weapons issued widely to Auxiliaries in
Herefordshire and Worcestershire

had served in the anti-terrorist section of the Shanghai police force before the
war and had put their knowledge at the disposal of the British Army. They were
influential in the revolutionary development of close combat fighting ('thuggery') using whatever weapons were available. The first contract for the manufacture of this famous fighting knife was given to the Wilkinson Sword
Company in January 1941. The knife and its sheath could be attached to the

leather waist belt or, by using the leather tabs on either side of the sheath, to the battle dress sleeve or leg.

In addition to its close combat role, the fighting knife had a more gruesome use. At least two of the Auxiliers recall that they were instructed to 'paunch' enemy sentries; that is, to disembowel them. The reason for this was to strike terror into the German forces, but this would also have rebounded on the local population and any captured Auxiliers. Knowledge today of the reaction to, for example, Maquis operations in June 1944 in France by the élite Waffen SS 'Das Reich' Division leaves no doubt that retribution would have been brutal in the extreme.

The patrols were also supplied with knuckledusters, garottes and a type of club officially called a 'knobkerrie' for close combat and the silent elimination of sentries. The influence of Fairbairn and Sykes also led to the training of patrols in unarmed combat where fists, boots and knees would be used. In 1940 this was revolutionary, but much of what was taught is now current practice in modern armed forces.

Joe King of Samson Patrol armed with a fearsome club, Joe refers to it as a shilelagh, although official documents refer to similar devices as 'knobkerries',
(Courtesy of Joe King)

In 1940 Churchill had written upon a memorandum concerning the setting up of the Units, 'These men must have revolvers'. And so they did have them. In Herefordshire and Worcestershire most men received the US Smith and Wesson .38, although a variety of other revolvers and pistols were to be used — the British Government had ordered over a million revolvers in 1940 at an advantageous price from the United States. In general military use the revolver fired a jacketed bullet rather than the .38 Special bullet in order to comply with the Hague Convention. The higher-powered special round fired a lead, round-nosed bullet. Because of the tendency of the bullet to expand on impact and so produce larger flesh wounds it was considered by the British Army to be outside the remit of the Convention which had proscribed the use of 'inhuman' weapons. However, the Special ammunition *was* made available to Auxiliers and many were officially converted (at Coleshill?) into dumdum bullets by the removal of the tip. If they had used such ammunition the Auxilier would have put himself beyond the terms of the Convention, although in practical terms this is unlikely to have made any difference as captured patrol members could only have expected summary justice.

Each patrol was given a .45 Thompson M1928A1 sub-machinegun—the famous Tommy gun—and this was usually given to the patrol sergeant. A very reliable, well made and hard hitting weapon, the Tommy gun was felt by some to be a little too heavy for their work, although on the whole it was welcomed as a boost to patrol firepower. This gun was reluctantly given up when the Sten gun became available in 1942. Like the Smith and Wesson revolver, the Thompson had formed part of the parcel of orders given to US manufacturers in the Summer of 1940; over a million were ordered. The gun could use either a 50 round drum magazine or the more commonly seen 20 round box magazine.

The 9mm Sten sub-machinegun was crude but effective. Prone to jamming and to accidental firing when dropped, it was nevertheless devastating when fired. A 32-

All-In Fighting *by Captain W.E. Fairbairn. Widely distributed during the war, it detailed a variety of close-combat attack and defence methods. Captains Fairbairn and Sykes, late of the Shanghai Police, were instrumental in developing the techniques used by the Units, Commandos, SOE, OSS and other special forces in the war. (Bernard Lowry Collection)*

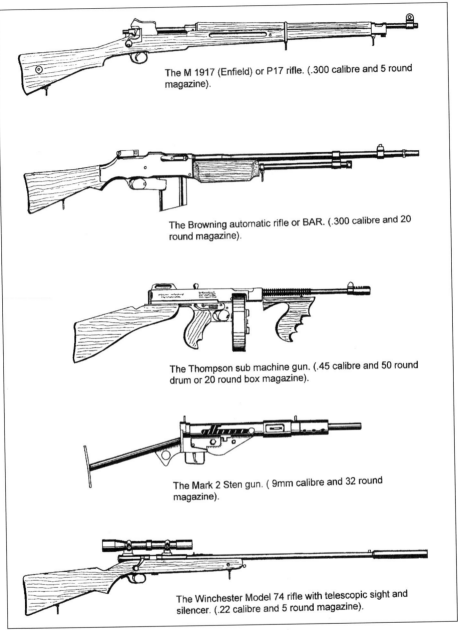

The M 1917 (Enfield) or P17 rifle. (.300 calibre and 5 round magazine).

The Browning automatic rifle or BAR. (.300 calibre and 20 round magazine).

The Thompson sub machine gun. (.45 calibre and 50 round drum or 20 round box magazine).

The Mark 2 Sten gun. (9mm calibre and 32 round magazine).

The Winchester Model 74 rifle with telescopic sight and silencer. (.22 calibre and 5 round magazine).

Small arms issued to Auxiliary patrols in Herefordshire and Worcestershire

round magazine and the ability of this relatively light weapon to be broken down for carriage made it an ideal weapon for the patrols and it supplemented the firepower for auxiliers previously armed only with revolvers or pistols. Many thousands would also be dropped to continental resistance groups, as

Ron Seymour of Samson patrol with the patrol's Thompson sub-machinegun. He is lying on a number of groundsheets and his gun lacks a magazine. No insignia is visible on his battle dress. (Courtesy of Ron Seymour)

well as arming members of the Home Guard and Army. The weapon could also be used to fire single shots.

Another automatic weapon issued was the US .30 M1918 Browning Automatic Rifle (BAR), also issued to the Home Guard. With a magazine holding 20 rounds it was a hard-hitting weapon but was probably too large and unwieldy for Auxiliary Unit purposes and its issue may not have been universal amongst the patrols. At least one local patrol had one as Dick Philips in Worcestershire was armed with this weapon.

For the silent elimination of sentries, tracker dogs and other targets requiring silence, patrols were issued with the US Winchester Model 74 .22 rifle. The British added an Enfield telescopic sight and a Parker-Hale silencer, the fitting probably taking place at workshops in the grounds of Coleshill House. The weapon could also double as a game rifle to supplement rations. The usefulness of this weapon was doubted by some patrols due to the delicate nature of the sights, and the rough usage it would have received on operations.

The standard rifle of the Home Guard, the US .30 M1917 (Enfield), more familiarly known as the 'P17, or 'Springfield' was issued on the basis of one or two per patrol. Over a million of these weapons arrived in July 1940, the British Government commissioning special trains to get them and their ammunition to the Home Guard and newly formed Auxiliary Units.

Other weapons intended for defence and carried by the patrol members were the No.36M fragmentation grenade (Mills Bomb) and the No.77 smoke grenade. The former had a four seconds fuse and the latter an 'all ways' impact fuse. Both required the need to take cover to avoid fragmentation splinters or the particles of burning white phosphorous from the smoke grenade.

For the destruction of tanks, stores or vehicle parks the No.74 ST and No. 76 SIP grenades were supplied. The former, also known as the Sticky Bomb, consisted of a glass flask of nitro-glycerine attached to a throwing handle containing the fuse. The flask was covered in a birdlime adhesive beneath detachable metal covers. In action the covers sprang off revealing the adhesive which was designed to stick to the surface of a tank on being thrown or placed. However, the tank's surface had to be free of mud, which rather limited the effectiveness of the grenade. An alternative use was as a demolition charge where the high explosive charge was extremely effective. Borne out of the desperate times in 1940, the No.74 had

The late Reg Wilkinson of the Worcestershire Overbury patrol with his US P17 rifle. He is dressed in Home Guard uniform complete with leather belt and gaiters. (Courtesy of the family of the late Reg Wilkinson)

certain drawbacks for its user. The nitro-glycerine content was prone to leakage after a time, and the tenacious adhesive cover could equally stick to the user's battledress as to an enemy tank.

The No. 76 SIP (Self-Igniting Phosphorous) grenade also required the user to be perilously close to his intended target. A rather more sophisticated version of the Molotov Cocktail, the No.76 consisted of a glass bottle, closed by a stopper, containing benzine, rubber and a small amount of phosphorous isolated from the other contents by a layer of water. Once the bottle broke, the phosphorous on contact with air ignited the inflammable mixture producing a dense blaze. Originally designed as an anti-tank weapon it could also be used as an incendiary bomb for the destruction of materiel. An alternative name was 'AW Bomb' after the manufacturers of the phosphorous, Albright and Wilson of Oldbury. In time, delayed action incendiary mines would also become available.

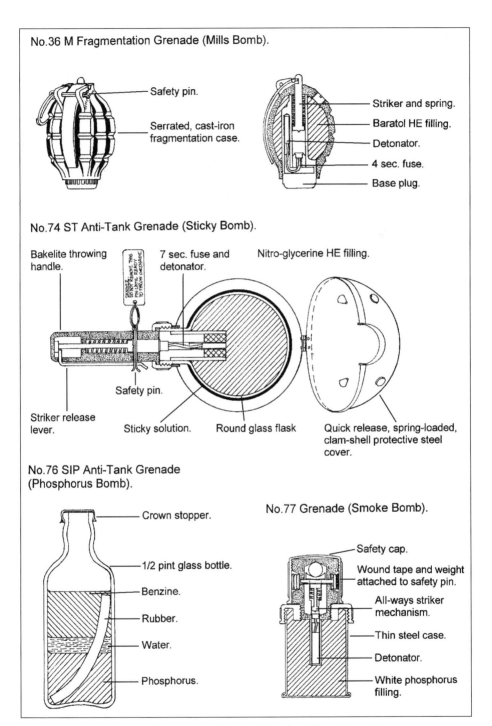

No.36 M Fragmentation Grenade (Mills Bomb).

Safety pin.

Serrated, cast-iron fragmentation case.

Striker and spring.

Baratol HE filling.

Detonator.

4 sec. fuse.

Base plug.

No.74 ST Anti-Tank Grenade (Sticky Bomb).

Bakelite throwing handle.

7 sec. fuse and detonator.

Nitro-glycerine HE filling.

Safety pin.

Striker release lever.

Sticky solution.

Round glass flask

Quick release, spring-loaded, clam-shell protective steel cover.

No.76 SIP Anti-Tank Grenade (Phosphorus Bomb).

Crown stopper.

1/2 pint glass bottle.

Benzine.

Rubber.

Water.

Phosphorus.

No.77 Grenade (Smoke Bomb).

Safety cap.

Wound tape and weight attached to safety pin.

All-ways striker mechanism.

Thin steel case.

Detonator.

White phosphorus filling.

Grenades or Bombs issued to Auxiliary Patrols

Explosives

The most remarkable aspect of the Units' armoury was the wide variety of sabotage material, many of the items being newly designed and introduced. The Units were amongst the first to receive the newly developed plastic explosive, available from the summer of 1940, 'plastic' referring to the malleable quality of the material—powerful RDX explosive mixed with beeswax or oil.

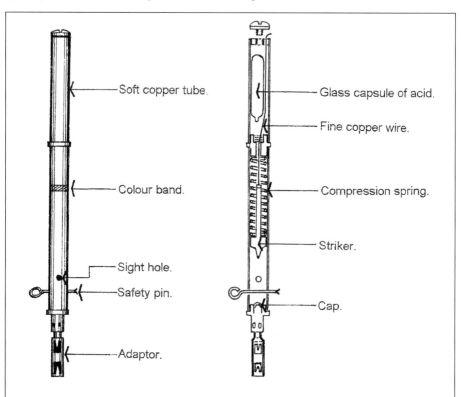

Time pencils were supplied with varying lengths of time delay. This time delay was indicated by a coloured band on the side of the pencil: red for 1/2 hour, white for 1 1/2 hours, green for 5 hours, yellow for 10 hours and blue for 20 hours. Temperature affected the time delay and these are the approximate times for the summer. In the winter the time delay could be extended by up to 50% more.

Auxiliaries were recommended to use two time pencils of the appropriate delay for each charge to ensure success. To activate the time pencil, the soft copper tube was to be squashed, not bent, in order to break the acid capsule. The acid would then slowly eat its way through the fine wire, which would part and release the striker. This in turn would fire the cap and activate the attached fuse or detonator and the charge.

The Time Pencil

Wrapped around a horseshoe-shaped magnet together with a time pencil and detonator a readymade anti-tank weapon could be fashioned, for placed against a tank driving wheel the resulting explosion would disable any tank. This extemporised weapon would lead to the magnetic clam and limpet mines: the latter was used in 1942 by the Royal Marines in Operation Frankton, the successful raid on German shipping in Bordeaux harbour. Plastic explosive could also be formed to match the profile of a rail and, attached with a smear of Vaseline, it made an effective railway-busting weapon. Overseas resistance groups, especially those in France in the summer of 1944, put this into practice with devastating results.

In addition to 'plastic', other commercial explosives were used such as Nobel's 808 and Polar blasting gelignite. However, these did not match the versatility and safety of the revolutionary new explosive.

A further new item was the acid delay time pencil fuse. Developed in Poland before the war, this fuse worked on the basis of the time taken for an acid contained in a crushable glass ampoule to eat through a gauge of copper wire. Once the wire broke a spring was released initiating a detonator or detonating cord. The thicker the wire, the longer was the delay. The action was also dependent on ambient temperatures and so fuses were colour coded to give delays at varying temperatures, hence the inclusion of a thermometer in the sabotage packs. In practice it was found that the acid delay fuse was unreliable and so later practice was to use two such fuses. An attempt on Hitler's life in March 1943 by dissident German officers using captured SOE acid delay time pencils, failed because only one, non-functioning, fuse was used. A later, more reliable fuse, the L (lead)-delay would be introduced but whether this was issued to the Auxiliary Units is not clear. This fuse worked on the principle of the time taken for a tellurium lead cylinder to break under the tension of a spring.

A range of fuse cords were supplied including Cordtex, Bickford and instantaneous in the explosives and incendiary materials packs known as 'Small Aux Units', 'Aux Units MkI' or 'Aux Units MkII'. In addition, the packs included insulating tape for preparing explosive charges and crimping tools for attaching fuse cord to time pencils. A range of anti-personnel devices was also provided including mines, pull and pressure switches. Amongst these was the AP switch, also known as the 'castrator'. This unpleasant weapon, when trodden upon, shot a bullet vertically towards the body. In addition, tyre burster mines would disable the largest enemy wheeled vehicles. *The Countryman's Diary 1939* instructed the Auxilier on the use of all of the above material, and also showed him how to produce extemporised mines and bombs.

As an example of one man's armoury, Guy Sainsbury of the Ross-on-Wye patrol wrote on the back of a War Office pamphlet a list of stores:

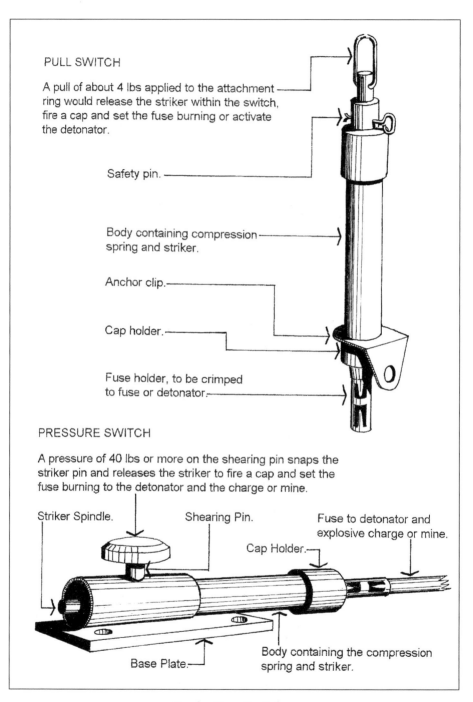

PULL SWITCH

A pull of about 4 lbs applied to the attachment ring would release the striker within the switch, fire a cap and set the fuse burning or activate the detonator.

Safety pin.

Body containing compression spring and striker.

Anchor clip.

Cap holder.

Fuse holder, to be crimped to fuse or detonator.

PRESSURE SWITCH

A pressure of 40 lbs or more on the shearing pin snaps the striker pin and releases the striker to fire a cap and set the fuse burning to the detonator and the charge or mine.

Striker Spindle.

Shearing Pin.

Fuse to detonator and explosive charge or mine.

Cap Holder.

Base Plate.

Body containing the compression spring and striker.

Booby Trap Switches

1 case ST (Sticky Bombs)
6 Mills (36M) (hand grenades)
16 sticks PBG (Polar blasting gelignite)
6 sticks plastic (explosive)
2 tins half hour time pencils
3 rolls insulation tape
1 smoke bomb
12 large incendiaries

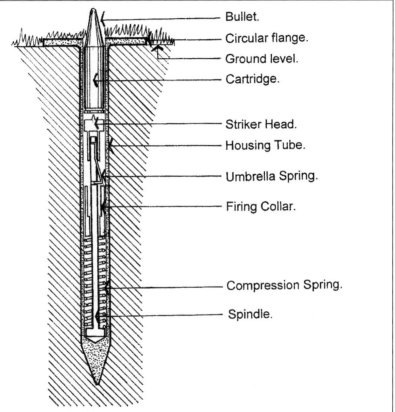

The A P Switch was supplied to Auxiliary patrols for use as a miniature anti-personnel mine. The device would be set into the surface of a footpath used by enemy sentries. It would be pushed into the ground up to the flange so that only the head of the bullet protruded. A person subsequently treading on the bullet would compress the umbrella spring, release the firing collar, which, under pressure from the compression spring, would push the striker head into the cartridge and fire the bullet. The A P Switch was intended to disable and demoralise enemy troops. It was known as the "castrator" to the Auxiliaries!

The Anti-Personnel or AP Switch

Once the Auxiliary Units had been stood down, the patrols' main explosive stores are believed to have been destroyed by the Royal Engineers as there was a risk of explosives such as gelignite becoming unstable. However, destruction was not complete, and individuals often retained small quantities of ammunition or explosives wittingly or unwittingly in barns or outbuildings and some may still remain today, yet to be discovered.

CHAPTER 7
Auxiliary Patrols in Herefordshire

Men recruited, principally, from the county's farming community manned the six Herefordshire patrols. The known or postulated locations of the Operational Bases suggest that, in addition to night harassment, the patrols were also positioned to block by sabotage action the principal roads and railways which converged on Hereford from the south and west, or led from Hereford into Worcestershire. Other possible targets included airfields, headquarters and fuel and ammunition dumps.

Adam Patrol

A surviving member of Adam Patrol, situated to the west of Hereford, is Geoffrey Morgan-Jones of Sugwas:

> At about the time of the Dunkirk evacuation in June 1940 I received a telephone call asking if I was willing to volunteer to do something to help my country. I had already volunteered to join the Local Defence Volunteers [later the Home Guard] when I returned to Britain from Australia in 1940.
>
> It is difficult for people now to realise how serious was the threat of invasion in the summer of 1940 and the desperate state of the country at that time.
>
> I was asked to go to Old Letton Court, the home of Alex Beck who would become the patrol sergeant. He was a farmer and in the First World War had won the DFC for shooting down an enemy aeroplane whilst serving in the Royal Flying Corps. Not only had he shot it down, but he had also walked into no-man's land to retrieve a part of the wing of the aircraft. This hung in a pride of place at the Court. I had a high opinion of the man. The members of my patrol, code named Adam, had known each other before the war. John Turner, our corporal, was later to be my best man, Evans was a friend and Beck and I hunted. Beach-Thomas, an engineer with Bulmers and somewhat on the outside of the group, had a writer father, Sir William Beach-Thomas. We were a well-chosen group who could also act individually.

Adam Patrol.
From left to right: Albert Pettifer, Leslie Evans, Geoffrey Morgan-Jones,
'Hughie' Hall, Alex Beck, Vernon Beach-Thomas and John Turner. Pettifer, as
Quartermaster Sergeant, was not part of the patrol, although it is possible
that, in the event of an emergency, both Pettifer and Lacon might have joined
this particular patrol. Beck wears his First World War 'wings' and Beach-
Thomas carried a fighting knife, although this does not appear to be of the
Fairbairn-Sykes variety. (Courtesy of Geoffrey Morgan-Jones)

I believe our patrol was one of the first to be established in the county. At this stage we had no Operational Base, being expected to fight from whatever cover we could find if an invasion took place. Later we each had a set of sabotage equipment and, once the invasion had started, we would gather together to plan our action and go off individually to commit sabotage. We were given weapons, including a Tommy gun and a revolver for each man.

Eventually our Operational Base was built in a wooded area within operating distance of old Letton Court but we never approached it in daylight. This was underground and had a corrugated iron roof and a small boarded escape tunnel, the exit from which I considered too close to the OB to be effective. The entrance to it was via a trapdoor covered by earth. I considered that the Royal Engineers had done a brilliant job in its construction especially as there was no sign of any spoil. Lighting was by candle but when this went out one night we realised that lack of oxygen was going to be a problem during long stays and we decided to find an alternative Base. One was established in some caves at Credenhill.

Near the OB was a separate underground explosives store, entered via a trap door. It contained time pencils, Mills grenades (No 36M), nitro-glycerine, and phosphorous bombs etc. We also had plenty of Sticky Bombs. Alex Beck experimented with one of these 'boosted' with plastic explosive. The force of the explosion damaged a cottage porch and brought out the Hay Civil Defence Corps who thought a bomb had landed in the area.

I vividly remember our first demonstration in the use of plastic explosive [PE]. An RE officer put a 'T'–shaped charge on a traction engine wheel—when detonated this left a T-shaped hole on the wheel. Another device was a magnet around which could be fitted PE and stuck to the sprocket wheel on the enemy tank. We were trained so that we could assemble explosive charges in the dark. Night firing was also practised.

When we went to Coleshill House we slept in a straw filled loft. To those of us who had been to public schools, such uncomfortable 'beds' were no problem. We were given lessons in unarmed combat and the use of the fighting knife for killing sentries. Major Todd's instructions were that, after killing, they were to be disembowelled. Further unarmed combat training was carried out by an instructor who visited Hereford. I remember one lesson taught us how to strike a sentry using a matchbox gripped in the palm of the hand.

Alex Beck also gave us training and some exercises were carried out at Holmer Grange where there was a pool. This was the home of 'Hughie' Hall, our Group Leader. At the time of D-Day the chance of going to France was mentioned if things were to go wrong there, but this never materialised further.

As for our operational role, Todd told us that it was to be 'a bloody nuisance to Gerry!', especially to keep them awake as this would affect their fighting efficiency. Otherwise, I don't remember any other role being explained. We did not know the location of the other patrols' OBs although we met other Auxiliers on exercises. If caught, we were to get a message to Alex Beck's wife. The whole basis was the less we knew the less we could disclose if captured. In the event of capture we had no illusions about our fate and we realised that the Germans would take reprisals against our families, too.

To keep us trained, exercises were held. I remember one where we had to 'booby trap' a high-ranking officer's car. Fortunately one of the patrol members created an unplanned but successful diversion by upsetting a hen house and its contents! This same person also tripped over a trip wire attached to an igniter and explosive. Fortunately a one-minute delay Bickford fuse was used so there was a slight delay and no one was hurt. As the war situation improved, we spent less time training but still managed to get together socially.

Another exercise involved the noting of a number on a 5-gallon drum guarded by an Army detachment in woods near Canon or King's Pyon. A member of our section got the number and carried off the drum as well, avoiding a nearby sentry by lying in a ditch. Our Intelligence Officer, Captain Christopher Sandford, however, was not happy with our initiative and we were reprimanded. Otherwise, I had little contact with Sandford. Other 'Adam' exercises involved the demolition of trees by explosives to block roads and exercises to test the security of Shobdon airfield.

A cocktail party at Bullingham Barracks, Hereford, started another operation. One of the Regular Army officers there refused to believe that anyone could break into a properly guarded camp. Alex decided to teach them a lesson! We drove to a spot at 2 a.m. and waited an hour to get sufficient night vision and, avoiding the sentries who were on patrol duty, entered the tented camp at Belmont at different points where we placed a thunderflash with a time pencil delay and other reminders of 'enemy presence'.

In June 1944 we were sent to the Isle of Wight for ten days, transported in a Bedford truck and staff car, and attached to an AA battery where we did night patrol work. Perhaps there was a fear of German diversionary raids but nothing happened.

The secrecy surrounding our patrol was never compromised. If we had discovered anyone who had breached this secrecy they would have been eliminated as soon as the invasion occurred.

Geoffrey Morgan-Jones' account provides some clues as to the operational role of 'Adam' in the event of an invasion. It seems likely that Shobdon airfield, to the north of the patrol, would have been a target in the event of it being captured by the Germans. Their aim would be to destroy enemy aircraft and

Geoffrey Morgan-Jones
(Bernard Lowry)

fuel and ammunition dumps on the airfield. Situated to the west of Hereford, the main roads and, especially, the railway line from South Wales would also have been targetted. In addition, the patrol would have generally made life difficult for the invader.

Abednigo Patrol

Situated between Hereford and Leominster, Abednigo Patrol was led by the patrol's sergeant, Richard Holford of Newton near Leominster. Its members, apart from Geoffrey Chambers and possibly Robert Brooks, were farmers. Chambers was the patrol corporal and his son, Adrian, remembers his father having .45 bullets for his Tommy gun and a Fairbairn-Sykes fighting knife. Chambers was a partner and livestock auctioneer at the Leominster firm of Russell, Baldwin and Bright and during the war was the local representative of the Wool Marketing Board.

Mary Morris is the daughter of another patrol member, Frank Hancorn, then a farmer at Eyton Court, where her husband now farms. Her father had started his working life at sea, but a bad fracture of his leg left him with a severe limp. Leaving the sea he had worked as a seed salesman, eventually moving to and buying the farm at Eyton Court. Like the relatives of the other Herefordshire Units' members she was told little of her father's wartime activities. After the war she remembers a type of explosive mine being discovered in the cellar and packets of nitro-glycerine being found in the cider mill. Some of these wartime supplies may have been used after the war to remove a tree, this narrowly missing a Mr Frank Dale.

Other members were Neston Capper and Geoffrey Thomas. Thomas's son, also called Geoffrey, records that during the war his father was a builder and agricultural contractor. In addition he farmed 21 acres of land, where a cache of Sticky Bombs were found after the war and which the Royal Engineers were called to remove. The patrol's principal target is likely to have been the railway line which ran north through the Dinmore Tunnel—a train derailed in a tunnel is a difficult obstacle to remove, and the main A49 over Dinmore Hill. Their OB is believed to have been situated on the flank of the hill.

Abednigo Patrol.
From left to right: Neston Capper, Robert Brooks, Geoffrey Thomas,
Geoffrey Chambers, Richard Holford and Frank Hancorn. Hancorn, for the
photograph at least, retains his revolver, together with its lanyard
and leather holster. (Courtesy of Mary Morris)

Jacob Patrol

John Thornton, former member of
Jacob Patrol, April 2001
(Mick Wilks)

To the east of 'Abednigo' was Jacob Patrol, whose OB was located in Warren Wood on the Bromyard Downs. From here the roads and railway into Worcestershire via the Teme Valley could be kept under observation.

Mrs Joan Bemand's father, John Hartwright, was the patrol corporal. She was told little about his role but remembers sleeping during the war with a box of grenades under her bed! One of 12 children, and born in 1899, John Hartwright was one of the older members of the patrols. He had served in the First World War in the Royal Horse Artillery and was therefore a natural choice for the post of corporal. He was not a farmer but worked as a lorry driver and mechanic for Fowlers of Bishops Frome. Other members were in farming. Mrs Jeanne Potter, widow of patrol member John Essex Potter, remembers her late husband having visited Wiltshire (presumably Coleshill House) whilst she was serving in the ATS in that county. His attempts to meet up with his future wife at the time had proved fruitless, however. She remembers John, a tall, strong man, as being an excellent shot whilst on his parent's large farm from where, as a child, he would ride by pony to the local school at Bromyard. John's brother Bill, remembers John going to the Isle of Wight, and being told of the Operational Base on the Bromyard Downs. Training of the patrol took place at a cider works; Bill Potter thought that this was at Bulmer's cider works, but presumably it was Watkin's at Holmer where the Group Leader 'Hughie' Hall lived and worked.

The patrol sergeant was Edward Heath Agnew, a farmer. An Oxford Rowing Blue, Agnew had taken over Brookhouse Farm, purchased for him by his grandparents, before the war, probably on leaving university. Like John Potter, Agnew would leave farming after the war: Agnew for a career in teaching at a private school, Potter going into the then new launderette business. Other members were William Farmer Pudge, a hop farmer, and David Went. Another member was John Thornton who has given an account of his time with 'Jacob':

> I joined the LDV/ Home Guard at the Police Station in Bromyard in May 1940 and was involved in patrolling Church Road in Stanford Bishop in the early stages of my service. The church stands in a prominent position from where it is possible to observe a large area of countryside and it became the site of our observation post. A tin shed at the back of the church provided shelter and we could sleep on bags of straw. The Home Guard commander was Captain Bradshaw-Janner and the HQ was in the village hall. I was issued with a Lee Enfield .303 rifle and five rounds of ammunition. This was kept at my home, the Stonehouse at Burley. I worked for Heath Agnew who then lived at Brookhouse Farm a couple of miles to the south of Bromyard.
>
> In the late summer or autumn of 1940 Agnew asked me whether I would like to join the Auxiliary Units. This was at about the time of a Home Guard dance at Stanford Bishop that he had organised. He told me that this would be the last thing that we would do in the Home Guard. I retained my uniform although I would later add the 'HFD 202' flashes.
>
> I believe that it was Captain Todd who had approached Agnew about forming an Auxiliary Units patrol and I was probably the first person to be asked to join Jacob Patrol. At the patrol's first meeting at Brookhouse Farm we were introduced to Todd. I formed the impression that he was very officious and it was best not to get on the wrong side of him. He

Jacob Patrol.
From left to right: David Went, John Thornton, John Hartwright,
William Pudge and John Potter. Missing from the photograph is the patrol
sergeant, Edward Heath Agnew. The men carry revolvers in standard
Army '37 pattern webbing holsters. (Courtesy of Jeanne Potter)

explained our role in the event of an invasion and gave us 48 hours to decide if we wished to join the Units. We then had to sign the Official Secrets Act and swear on a small Bible that we would keep our new role secret. He told us that we had to do as much damage to the Germans before they killed us. If caught, we were told that we were on our own!

At the first meeting were Trevor Parker, a big hop grower from Cheney Court, John Hartwright, Howard Kelsey, William Farmer Pudge from Bishops Frome and David Went from Pencombe. I think Trevor Parker was made second-in-command but he tended to kick over the traces and eventually left. John Hartwright then took his place. There was also a fellow called Robinson, a schoolteacher from Bromyard. He was reprimanded for talking about us in a pub and left to join the RAF.

My initial training was at Coleshill. Howard Kelsey and I travelled there together by car, the final part of the journey was in an Army lorry. The training included unarmed combat and I can remember the instructor telling me to put him in a stranglehold from behind. The next thing I knew was that I was on the ground several yards away. They damn near crippled us! I went to Coleshill three times and I can remember meeting Peter Price, the former boxer from Worcester, who was part of the staff there. On one of the later visits I was involved in a night patrol and on the last visit there were hordes of patrols there. [These later visits were almost certainly to participate in competitions].

One of the first things we did after formation was to go to Credenhill Camp to have tetanus jabs but unfortunately mine did not take after two attempts. I came out in boils each time and when I complained Todd gave me a pound note for my trouble. He suggested that Agnew should match it but he wouldn't. It was more than my wages at the time.

We also went to Credenhill for grenade training. They had a proper range there and we were told that if we dropped one *we* would have to sort it out for ourselves—*they* weren't going to help us. The target was a boulting of straw at about 20 yards range. When the grenade hit it and exploded, the boulting would disintegrate and be replaced by another one. We also had gas training there in the gas chamber: pinching our noses we tried to avoid breathing the gas which was, I believe, phosgene.

The patrol had a Thompson sub-machinegun with which we practised firing bursts or single shots. Some of the patrol seemed to be nervous of the weapon and would close their eyes when firing. I had my first gun, a .410 shotgun, when I was 10 so I was used to guns. Firing and stripping down and re-assembling the Tommy gun in the dark was no trouble to me. However, you had to be extremely careful as a lost part meant an inoperable weapon, and no spares were available. We were each issued with a .38 Smith and Wesson revolver and a Fairbairn-Sykes fighting knife. We were also issued with a different type of knife which had a curved end. [These were probably tyre slashers later issued to SOE agents]. For the revolver we had standard and dumdum rounds: three of each were in the chamber in alternate order. [John's wife Nessie also fired the revolver, which was kept at home, and she remembers that it had a terrific kick]. I also had a knuckleduster that I kept for a long time after the war.

Our firearms practice range was on Heath Agnew's farm, in a secluded position down in the bottom, where we would fire up into a high bank in the corner of Brookhouse Wood. We took it in turns with the targets and would signal back to those firing to indicate their scores. There was a large hole where the targets were situated protecting those operating the flags. On other occasions we would use the same hole for explosives practice. We also went to a quarry owned by the Holland-Martin family at Overbury Court where we had practice with explosives and different types of weapons. I can also remember a gathering of patrols at Overbury Court: this was the last time I saw Captain Todd before he went overseas. He was asking for volunteers to go to Norway with him and two put their names forward, one of them being Heath Agnew but he did not go. [The reason for the request may lie in that Winston Churchill, in 1942, was interested in an invasion of northern Norway in aid of the Soviet Union and thence 'rolling back' the Nazis. Churchill may have seen a role for the Auxiliary Units in destroying aircraft, fuel and ammunition dumps, but the plan was deemed impractical by the chiefs of staff. Jim Griffin of Jehu patrol in Worcestershire also remembers their patrol being asked the same question.]

Our HQ for meetings was Heath Agnew's home at Brookhouse Farm. When he moved to Yarkhill we met at the Hop Pole at Bromyard. This did not please me being a teetotaller, especially as, when I moved to Mr Saunders' farm at Suckley, it involved a seven miles cycle ride. As the pressure eased, the meetings became more of a social event. I remember meeting the Ross patrol in Monmouth: they had a good meal and when we drove through Ross we let off thunderflashes which got the Home Guard out!

Two Operational Bases were built, both in Warren Wood overlooking the racecourse on Bromyard Downs. The first was L-shaped and built of concrete blocks but it was too small. With six of us in there it was very claustrophobic and we had problems with fumes. We asked for another one to be built. At that time we stored our explosives in the large outbuilding next to the oasthouse at Brookhouse Farm.

The second OB was built some distance away from the first. It was at the top of the wood, near the reservoir and I believe that it was still there two years ago. It may still contain the bunks. [Subsequent inspection shows that it has been destroyed and the hole filled in.] It was built of corrugated iron with a brick, 20 feet long, escape tunnel. The builder was a local contractor who was helped by the bailiff's men. The tunnel emerged between two large rocks in a quarry. We were not too happy with the original hinged entrance so we made our own with counterbalance weights and covered it with tree grease so that leaves and twigs would stick to it and disguise it. The bailiff was always prying into our affairs which was a worry to us and at one stage he started to mark the

The Hop Pole Hotel, Bromyard. This was the unofficial headquarters and meeting place for Jacob Patrol after Haath Agnew had moved to Yarkhill. (Mick Wilks)

trees around our OB for felling. I telephoned Heath Agnew and he managed to get this stopped. The bailiff was not happy but any felling would have exposed the OB. Incidentally, I had a great deal of respect for Agnew. He was an outstanding leader and would not ask us do anything he would not do himself. For example, if any of the caches of explosive were starting to deteriorate he would inspect them himself rather than ask us.

We stayed at the OB at weekends, from Friday to Sunday. After three days we would be getting on each other's nerves and would be ready to leave. I found it particularly difficult to stay there for any length of time and always preferred to be above ground. One man was always outside keeping watch armed with the patrol .22 rifle. The .22 was usually loaded with the long bullets but we also had the short ammunition, too. There was a telephone in the OB connected via two wires to another one hidden under a yew tree near the road. From there the observer could watch the common and give warning of anyone approaching. The Downs would have made an ideal area for German camps, vehicle parks or fuel dumps.

For lighting we had two Kelly lamps, small, single wick paraffin lamps with a small glass bulb. Inside we had a store of food, mainly tinned, such as corned beef, peaches etc. We ate the food cold and raw and did not cook. Water could be obtained from a well on the downs and we intended to live off the land as far as we could. We also had a large, sealed, stoneware jar of rum. Despite the seal, the other patrol members drank the rum which looked like treacle. The jar was refilled with water and the seal replaced. We should have been shot for this because I think some of the more nervous members would have needed the rum to carry out operations if there had been an invasion.

Towards the end it became very damp and we had a rota for checking it a couple of times a week. However, not every member stuck to this system. The last time the patrol met was to take out the blankets and food that were then loaded onto an Army lorry, the armaments going to Yarkhill. The .22 went missing—we would all liked to have kept it—and the Army had to fetch it back from one of the patrol members.

When the second Operational Base was built, the original one became our explosives store. We had phosphorous grenades and Sticky Bombs that we buried in a couple of places. One was amongst the trees opposite Clater Park, near the main road past Brockhampton. We cut part of the way through some of the large beech trees by the road, and these would have been blown down by explosive to form a roadblock. Sticky Bombs would than have been thrown over the big wall by the road and onto enemy tanks below. The other bomb store was under a yew tree near the road across the common by Brockhampton School. We didn't mark either site but at the end of the war the bombs near the school were dug up, but I don't remember if the bombs near the main road were found. We thought the Germans might use the school as a billet and the old workhouse, a hospital, for their casualties. Both would have been attacked by our patrol.

[The trees opposite Clater Park might also have been used to trap German officers as follows.] One of our main tasks was to kill German officers as Todd had told us that if these were dealt with, the rest of the troops would be demoralised. We were to fell one of the beech trees across the road and when an enemy staff car came to a halt, another tree would be felled to prevent retreat. The occupants would then be killed with grenades. The trees that were cut through were felled at the end of the war, but you can still see the gap. If any of us had been injured during operations we were to make our way to either Mrs Harris or Mrs Lane, both of whom lived on the Downs, and they would look after us.

Heath Agnew sold Brookhouse Farm to the Cadburys and bought Castle Farm at Yarkhill where he kept Hereford Cattle. I then went to work for Colonel Lutley at The Warren and lived in White Railings Cottage on the Downs. From there I was able to keep an eye on the OBs and I would telephone Agnew once a week. It was particularly difficult for me during this period as I was working with two men who had helped to build the second OB. They constantly asked about our patrol in a casual way and said that they would tell the Germans where the OBs were. After the war they were shocked to learn that they would have been shot if there had been an invasion to prevent them giving away our locations.

We had a message 'postbox'. This was a loose stone in the wall around Brockhampton School, near the entrance into the school from the Downs where there used to be a fowl pen. We tried out the system three times and were supposed to get written messages back but we never did:

Clater Pitch, between Brockhampton and Clater Park. Site of a wartime Home Guard road block and potential ambush site of German staff cars by Jacob Patrol. The gap in the trees on the left of the road marks the site of beech trees, part cut through in preparation for such an ambush, and since felled. (Mick Wilks)

the original message would still be there. The original 'postman' was therefore dismissed and the school headmaster replaced him. Strangely enough he had a German name, Essenheim. The letters were addressed to HQ but we did not know where that was. [This system was very similar to the one set up in Worcestershire—see Chapter 8. There the messages were to go to the Group Leaders and it is likely that the same system prevailed in Herefordshire. The HQ referred to was probably at Eye Manor, the home of Captain Sandford].

Training exercises included night patrols, in twos, to Brockhampton and Buckinhill. [These are large houses in the Bromyard area almost certainly identified as potential German HQs]. There would be two of us up front with the others at ten yards intervals behind. We would always avoid the skyline as you would show up against the sky even at night. We would often watch for the Home Guard coming over the skyline. For night patrolling I wore a homemade Balaclava—the Home Guard service cap would catch in the bushes and fall off too easily to be of any use. We used mud on our faces and hands for camouflage. Our objectives always resulted in us crawling about in mud! I remember coming across some ferrets at Buckinhill. David Went wanted one, so he took one and let the rest loose. We were issued with rubber-soled sneakers or black pumps for night patrols but we preferred to wear our boots for going through mud. These were ordinary boots, not hobnailed like the normal Home Guard

John Thornton, former member of Jacob Patrol, indicating the loose stone in the wall around Brockhampton School which was the wartime 'dead letter drop' for the patrol. (Mick Wilks)

boot. We only had one uniform so we used to wear our working clothes for training.

Some of our training was at Holmer where there was a big lake. We had to run across a pontoon bridge there carrying all our equipment. One part of the bridge was mined and if you stepped there the bridge collapsed and you went in! If you didn't fall in, the instructors, a severe and bloodthirsty lot, pushed you in, and then you were wet all day. We also practised silent killing on a stuffed dummy mounted in a doorway on elastic bands. We were always trained to cut upwards with our knives, never downwards. This was to prevent the enemy grabbing your wrist and disarming you. After killing the enemy we were told by Todd to cut their 'knackers' off to demoralise the rest. Todd worked with the sergeants rather than the men when we were training. [The training location at Holmer may have been at Holmer Grange, the home of the Group Leader, Hall].

Brockhampton School on the Bromyard Downs, identified by Jacob Patrol as a potential billet for German occupying forces. The wartime headmaster became the patrol's courier. (Mick Wilks)

On one occasion six patrols assembled at a farm at Holmer belonging to Geoff Hoddell's brother, [this may be Leslie Hoddell who was a member of Caleb Patrol]. Geoff was a patrol leader. Each patrol had to place a magnet on farm implements stored in the fold yard and leave the patrol name on a piece of paper. I was the only one to get in without being spotted. I weighed only ten stones and could get through anything: barbed wire or fencing. I always thought crawling was not a good idea: you were too vulnerable to being bayonetted by a sentry. I always tried to stay on my feet using available cover as I could then defend myself. [This exercise was almost certainly part of a local competition to select a team to go on to Coleshill for a national event].

Another night exercise was at Stanford Court where John Potter lived. There we had to set off phosphorous bombs with timers to coincide with the appearance of the 'enemy'. We had an observer to warn us of their approach and at a certain point we would activate the timers, but they didn't always go off! We had moved our training area here after Agnew moved to Yarkhill. It was a problem clearing up after the exercises and finding bits and pieces in the dark—and how do you disguise scorched trees?

Some exercises were with the Home Guard. One involved getting into their tented camp at the top of New Road in Bromyard. Despite all of our training I could not march. Captain Sandford did try to instil some discipline in us but we were still civilians and did not take to it.

When I moved to Suckley I found it very difficult to ask for time off for training exercises. Going out several times a week including Sundays and doing night training messed up your home life. I had two small children to think of later, and I told my wife that in the event of an invasion she should bury some food in the garden as the first thing the Germans would do was to pinch all the food.

I did not go to the Isle of Wight but two other patrol members did go.

I have to question the recruiting policy for the Units as I think that more working men should have been included in the patrols. We were familiar with the countryside after dark, and getting around and killing things. It was a question of kill or be killed and I am not sure if all of the patrol members were up to it. Before I joined, my mate Hubert Yates and I would be out much of the night catching rabbits, badgers etc. I knew every inch of the countryside around Bromyard, which was useful when we did night exercises. I tried to get Hubert into the Auxiliaries but they would not accept him. He did join the Home Guard, however.

There were times when we got criticised for not doing more for the war effort but we couldn't talk about our role. I was actually called up for the regular forces but after a few days four or five of us were sent home. They obviously knew what we were involved in but it was never recognised, and afterwards we just wanted to be left alone. All we had to show for our efforts was the '202' lapel badge and the letter of thanks.

Mechach Patrol

To the south of Jacob Patrol was Mechach Patrol, led by Martin Hooton. A surviving member is William Roy Robinson:

In 1940 I was approached by Geoffrey Griffiths of Bosbury to join the Auxiliary Units. I was already in the Home Guard at the time. Our Group Leader was 'Hughie' Hall. It may have been at his home in Holmer that we practised crossing a pool on a rope. The Operational Base was below the ramparts of Wall Hills, a hill fort near Ledbury. We reached it by following a track into a wood where the underground bunker was situated. Our visits to our OB, which was on Ernie Barnet's land, one of our members, were not that frequent, perhaps once a month. On top of the hill fort was an observation post linked by a field telephone to the bunker. I cannot recollect what our precise role would have been in the event of an invasion, but I believe it may have been to disrupt the railway line near the Ledbury tunnel and viaduct. We held an exercise with the local Home Guard Battalion where we successfully 'captured' Ledbury station using thunderflashes to simulate grenades.

We were also taught how to immobilise an aircraft by sabotaging it with explosive placed on the tail or wing root. We also received training at Coleshill House where we slept in a large, barn-like building. We were advised not to smoke as below us was, allegedly, a million rounds of ammunition. We were trained there in night exercises, especially grenade throwing. It was at Coleshill that Geoff Griffiths, a lively individual and our corporal, played a prank by getting hold of a rooster at three o'clock in the morning and throwing it into the sergeants' Nissen hut. You can imagine the commotion! Geoff denied any involvement, saying that he was asleep at the time!

Our patrol sergeant was Martin Hooton, a schoolmaster who had been evacuated with Felstead School to Canon Frome Court. The remainder of the patrol farmed, apart from Fred Mayo who was the head groundsman on an estate. The atmosphere in the patrol was very informal and democratic.

I was initially given a Smith and Wesson revolver, the chamber of which had been enlarged to take a longer bullet. The Patrol also had a Tommy gun, later replaced by a Sten gun, and a .22 silenced sniper rifle. To put tracker dogs off the scent we were also issued with dog repellent powder. Four-second fused grenades were issued together with phosphorous bombs, plastic explosive and Polar blasting gelignite. This latter explosive was later withdrawn as it was considered to be too volatile. We received four different types of fuses plus 'mousetrap' booby traps. Most of us had been to private schools where there were Army cadet forces where we had learned to shoot; we would also shoot on the farms. I don't recollect being trained much in the use of the small arms — when we were issued with the Sten gun I took it home and practised in the fields.

Mechach Patrol.
From left to right: Edward Lewis, Fred Mayo, Ernest Barnet, Martin Hooton,
Geoffrey Griffiths, Roy Robinson and John Rhys-Thomas.
(Courtesy of Roy Robinson)

I remember Major Todd tearing down on our assembled group in
1941 to warn us that Moscow had only three weeks before it fell. Perhaps
he thought that the invasion of Britain might be 'on' again.

Another surviving member of 'Mechach' is 'Dick' Mayo. Sadly, his brother
Fred, also a member of the patrol passed away in 2001; they were christened
respectively Percy Pendry and Alfred Harry. Fred had joined the LDV in May
1940 and had been approached by Hooton to join the patrol. This choice may
have been because of his intimate knowledge of the countryside and especially
local footpaths. Dick Mayo now lives in Devon. Like his brother, he was in the
LDV in 1940 and joined at his suggestion. At that time he worked for a coal
delivery firm but was in the patrol a short time before being called up, finishing
the war as a tank driver in the European campaign. He remembers a lot of
emphasis on the Ledbury tunnel and railway line, but believes that patrol
members were told little about their role. He also recalls the times when he had
to crawl around on his belly and when a tree on Ted Lewis's land was blown to
pieces. This explosion was heard at his coal depot three miles away and was
believed to be a German bomb—of course, Mayo could not enlighten them!
John Thomas and Ted Lewis were the other two patrol members.

The Operational Base, built by the Army, was well provided with food and
beer, cooking being done on a Primus stove with lighting provided by a Tilley

Above: The late Fred Mayo (Mick Wilks)
Left: Roy Robinson (Bernard Lowry)

lamp. The local Home Guard, curious as to what the patrol were doing, did try to find the base but without success. Little contact was made with other patrols although he can remember being in a competition with the Ross (Shadrach) patrol.

Caleb Patrol

Close to Hereford was Caleb Patrol. It is believed that the patrol's Operational Base was on Dinedor Hill, as the summit of the hill would have given a good view of the roads and railways coming in to Hereford from South Wales and the Wye Valley. Such a position would have also given easy access to the Royal Ordnance Factory at Rotherwas, a site of value to the Germans if, in a retreat, the British Army had failed to totally destroy the installation and its contents.

Unfortunately there appear to be no survivors from this patrol, which was led by Sergeant Angus Wilson, a Hereford seed merchant who died during the course of the war. One of the other members was John Cleland who farmed at Dinedor. Some training may have been carried out at Lyde Court, Leslie Hoddell's farm. Ernest Tisdale and John Ryan, a veterinary surgeon from Hereford, together with Corporal Dennis Howard-Smith were the remaining members. Geoffrey Morgan-Jones of Adam Patrol believes that 'Caleb's' OB may have been compromised by the activities of an Army officer and his girl-friend. If this was the case, security would have been breached but whether a new OB was built elsewhere is not known. It is believed the officer was moved away from the area.

Caleb Patrol.
From left to right: John Cleland, Leslie Hoddell, Angus Wilson,
Denis Howard-Smith, John Ryan and Ernest Tisdale. The patrol sergeant,
Wilson, died during the war and a photograph of his face has been glued
on to a stand-in. No weapons are carried, but the photograph shows
Home Guard patches sewn into the upper arms of the battledress. No other
identifiable insignia is visible apart from Herefordshire Regiment cap badges.
(Courtesy of David Cleland)

Shadrach Patrol

The most southerly patrol was near Ross-on-Wye. Shadrach was led by Sergeant Frank Green who farmed at Huntsham Court near Symond's Yat. The patrol contained three members of the Sainsbury family, brothers who farmed at different locations in the area; Harry Sainsbury was the corporal, another brother being John Sainsbury. Charmingly recalled by another patrol's member as being 'as wild as hawks', they also had another farmer, Ted Price, in their patrol.

Guy Sainsbury had been a Special Constable at the start of the war and his senior police officer was not pleased when he had to relinquish his post on joining the Auxiliary Units. In common with other Auxiliers, Guy had talked little of his duties to his wife Denise, although he had divulged that, if there had been an invasion, two people in Ross were to be eliminated. Perhaps these people knew too much, or were considered to be potential Quislings? Like other Hereford Units' members, her husband had been sent to the Isle of Wight and had also attended courses, including unarmed combat for which he had also been issued with duplicated sheets on the subject of 'thuggery'.

Their Operational Base is believed to have been on Coppet Hill and close to the Symonds Yat and Welsh Bicknor railway tunnels. From this position the

Shadrach Patrol.
From left to right: John Sainsbury, Harry Sainsbury, Frank Green, Guy
Sainsbury and Edward Price. Green and Guy Sainsbury, lacking holsters,
have put their revolvers into the map pockets of their battledress trousers.
(Courtesy of Denise Sainsbury)

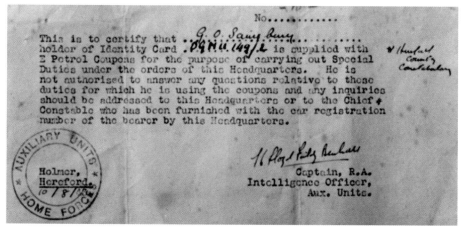

A letter of authority issued to Guy Sainsbury by Captain Lloyd Bucknall RA,
Intelligence Officer, and stamped 'Auxiliary Units Home Forces' at Holmer
on 10 August 1943. The letter states that the bearer is supplied with E Petrol
Coupons, is on 'Special Duties'—note the use of capital letters—and that he
is not authorised to answer any questions. Roy Robinson also possesses such
a letter, so it is likely that all vehicle drivers in the Units were issued with
similar letters in the event of their being stopped at police road checks.
(Courtesy of Denise Sainsbury)

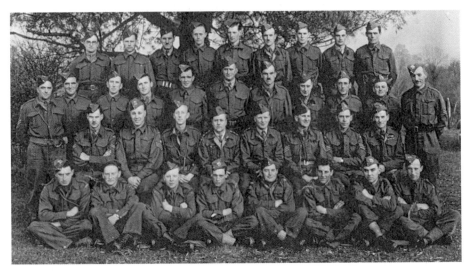

A group photograph taken of the Herefordshire patrols at standing down in late 1944. Also present are the Group Leaders, Captains Lacon and Hall. A number of the Auxiliers have the '202' badge sewn onto their battledress sleeves. The Hereford photographers Vivians took the group and individual patrol photographs. From left to right:
Back row: J.F. Ryan (Caleb), J. Rhys-Thomas (Mechach),
J.B. Sainsbury (Shadrach), W.R. Robinson (Mechach),
N.D.O. Capper (Abednigo), G.O. Sainsbury (Shadrach), J.E. Potter (Jacob),
G. Morgan-Jones (Adam), V. Beach-Thomas (Adam)
Third row: J.F. Hartwright (Jacob), E. Lewis (Mechach),
E.F. Barnet (Mechach), L.J. Hoddell (Caleb), G. Griffiths (Mechach),
J. Turner (Adam), H.E. Sainsbury (Shadrach), E.C. Tisdale (Caleb),
G.P. Thomas (Abednigo), F.J. Hancorn (Abednigo),
G.H. Chambers (Abednigo)
Second row: D. Howard-Smith (Caleb), A.T. Pettifer (QMS),
M.G. Hooton (Mechach), G.S.E. Lacon (Group Leader), J.H. Hall (Group Leader), F.W. Green (Shadrach), R.E. Holford (Abednigo), A. Beck (Adam)
Front row: D.T. Went (Jacob), J. Cleland (Caleb), W.F. Pudge (Jacob),
J. Thornton (Jacob), E.R. Price (Shadrach), L. Evans (Adam),
R.G.H. Brooks (Abednigo), F. Mayo (Mechach)
(Courtesy of Geoffrey Morgan-Jones)

patrol could have posed serious problems to the road and rail communications of an enemy coming up the river valley route.

Not apparently attached to any of the patrols, Sergeant Albert Pettifer of Hereford was the Group Quartermaster. It is not clear what training he received or if, once 'the balloon's gone up', he would have joined a patrol.

CHAPTER 8
Auxiliary Patrols in Worcestershire

Both documentary and anecdotal evidence indicate that there were at least six GHQ Auxiliary patrols formed in the Worcestershire countryside during the summer of 1940. The majority of recruits, as elsewhere, came from the farming community, but included amongst them were also country estate workers and boy scouts. A common factor in their recruitment was a keen sense of duty and an intimate knowledge of their locality. During the life of the patrols the personnel changed as the regular forces claimed men or others moved away to work elsewhere and were replaced, or the patrols simply diminished in size.

The operations of the six patrols for which there is clear evidence were coordinated initially by Captain John Todd, the first Intelligence Officer for the area. At an early stage this role of coordination was taken on by the van Moppes brothers and later Roger Smith, who was promoted to join them as a Group Commander. Thurston Holland-Martin seems also to have had a co-ordinating role in the early part of the Auxiliaries existence in Worcestershire. The Worcestershire Auxiliary Patrols are listed below in the likely order in which they were formed.

Samson Patrol
Probably because this patrol was recruited mainly from Boy Scouts from Broadheath who were only 17 or so years old at the time, there are more former members of the patrol still living and their memories are sharper than most. Much anecdotal evidence has therefore been collected about the patrol and its activities. This was further added to at a reunion, in March 2001, of some of the former patrol members at the home of their former sergeant, Geoff Devereux, although precisely who was in the original patrol is still hotly debated!

Geoff, now living near Exeter but formerly of Broadheath, believes that his patrol was the first to be formed in Worcestershire, followed by Roger Smith's at Crowle. Geoff must therefore have been the first of the 40 or so Auxiliaries recruited in Worcestershire during 1940. He often wonders how he came to be chosen to lead the patrol and thinks that it may have been influenced by Dan Asterley, who was the Headmaster of Aymestrey School, at Crown East, and the local Home Guard commander. However, Geoff has a clear memory of the method of recruiting him and the formation of his patrol:

> I was brought up in the country. My father was a gamekeeper and from an early age I was a keen Boy Scout. In our village we had a wonderful Scout Master and by the time I was 15 I was a King's Scout with Bushman's Thong and Gold Cords. At 16, I was one of eight scouts selected to represent England at the World Jamboree in Wellington, New Zealand. We were scheduled to sail on the day that war broke out. I was also in the OTC at school.
>
> After matriculation, I joined an engineering company in Worcester as a student apprentice. I was surprised one morning to be called to the telephone. The caller asked for my full name and identity card number. He said: 'My name is Captain John Todd of the Intelligence Corps'. He then asked what was the time of my lunch break. I told him it was in 15 minutes' time. He said: 'Speak to no-one. Come to the main gate and you will see a black Pontiac parked across the road. With your identity card in your hand walk across the road and get into the car'. It can be imagined how nervous I was during those 15 minutes as I had never had any contact with the Intelligence Corps and could not imagine what they could possibly want to talk to me about. I was then still only 17 years of age.
>
> Plucking up my courage I went to the main gate and saw a black car parked across the road. I walked across, opened the door, got in and the car drove away. After a few minutes Captain Todd told me that he wanted to talk to me somewhere where our conversation would not be overheard and I directed him to a country lane. [Geoff has since said that they parked about half-way along Three Quarter Mile Lane, near Rushwick, to the west of Worcester]. He produced a small Bible and asked me to swear on it that I would abide by the Official Secrets Act. He then said that Mr Churchill was convinced that the Germans were about to invade the UK and that as a matter of extreme urgency a guerrilla force was to be recruited and trained to harass the invaders. I had been highly recommended to him and he asked if I would be prepared to recruit and lead the local operation. I was to meet him the next day with a list of possible recruits without any reference to them as the whole matter was to be treated with the utmost secrecy. I was returned to the office with instructions to repeat the procedure the next day—with the list. After handing this over he said that it would be necessary, in the event of an invasion, to have a secret base for our operations and that I should give careful thought to a suitable site. John Todd warned me that life expectancy would be likely to be approximately 15 days from the arrival of the Germans on our patch!

We met again the next day when he produced a dossier on each of the names I had given him and said that he approved the list and that I should go ahead and recruit them and that they were to be sworn in under the Official Secrets Act. John Todd instructed me on the procedure I should adopt for the swearing in of my friends and ensure that they were aware of the seriousness of the undertaking.

The reference to the life expectancy of the patrol being about two weeks, once the Germans had arrived, was a commonly held view and John Todd seems to have been at pains to ensure that the new recruits to the Auxiliaries were aware of this. Geoff Devereux tells us that, because his patrol were well trained, could trust each other and knew the locality intimately, this would give them a considerable advantage over the Germans. It was not their aim to confront the enemy, so the patrol were very confident about their role and had every intention of going on much longer than two weeks!

Geoff Devereux, former sergeant of Samson Patrol, photographed later in the war as a newly commissioned 'one pip wonder' in an anti-tank regiment of the Regular Army. (Courtesy of Geoff Devereux)

The membership of the initial patrol is, as noted above, still a matter of some debate amongst the survivors and there are no contemporary written records to confirm it precisely. However, the balance of evidence would indicate to us that it comprised Geoff Devereux (Sergeant and Patrol Leader), Rob Boaz, Val Clines, who was second in command of the patrol, Arch Clines, Joe King and Ron Seymour. Most were fellow members of the Broadheath Scout Troop. The one exception was Joe King, who was a cousin of Val Clines, lived close to Broadheath Common and was well known to the other village lads. The recruitment of this patrol can be dated to July/August 1940 because Joe King tells us that he celebrated his 18th birthday on 4 August, by which time he and Arch Clines were members of the patrol. Geoff Devereux tells us that John Todd, who became a friend of his family, and often called at their home at Broadheath, had said that Samson Patrol was the first to be recruited in the Midlands.

John Todd told Geoff that he would be provided with an underground Operational Base or OB and was asked to choose a suitable site. Geoff was at first dubious about using an OB which might prove to something of a trap for the patrol if it was discovered. Nevertheless, Captain Todd insisted and gave Geoff the site characteristics required. The site eventually chosen for their OB was in an area of extensive woodland which used to stand on the north side of the A44, between Cotheridge and Broadwas, Geoff marking out the plot with sticks. Regrettably, most of this woodland has been cleared and the land culti-vated leaving no sign of the OB, but apparently it survived for a period after the war when a number of children discovered it while exploring the woods. The location was chosen because it was intended to conduct sabotage operations against German occupation forces using the western approaches to Worcester, primarily the A4103, A44 and A443 and, most importantly, the railway.

Within a few days of choosing his OB site, Geoff Devereux remembers:

> The Managing Director of my company called me into his office and said that he had been officially requested to give me extended leave and within a few days I was on my way to GPO Highworth.
>
> I cannot remember how long I stayed at Coleshill but I certainly had training in the use of Plastic explosive, sticky bombs, phosphorous grenades, booby traps and field craft. I was issued there with a .32 auto-matic and ammunition, a .300 P17 American rifle and a Fairbairn dagger, and trained in their use.

The .32 automatic pistol issued to Geoff was of Italian make, possibly a Beretta. The journey to Coleshill can be dated fairly accurately as Geoff mentioned that the journey down to Highworth in the black Pontiac with John Todd, who was attending the same course, was a particularly painful trip. Geoff had received a shrapnel wound in his backside during the bombing raid on the Meco works, in St John's, Worcester, his place of employment, and as a result had to sit on one side of his bottom for the whole journey! This air raid by a single Junkers Ju 88 was on Thursday, 3 October 1940, and was four days before he travelled to Highworth.

After returning from Coleshill to Worcester by train, Geoff was subse-quently taken by John Todd to the now completed OB and he remembers being very impressed with the standard of construction and the efficient camouflage. His earlier misgivings about it being a trap were mollified and

> the six members of the patrol lived in the OB at weekends and sometimes during the week, when we did our [practice] night attacks on individual

vehicles and laagers. As we were all Boy Scouts [with the exception of Joe King] and most of us had poached the area, these night patrols were nothing new to us. In addition to my night exercises and having been in the OTC at school, I was able to instruct the patrol in the use of service equipment, rifles, grenades, etc., as well as pass on the training I had received at Coleshill. We also had a local Army PE instructor who advised us on keeping fit and unarmed combat.

We were mainly senior Boy Scouts and after the Scout Master had gone back in the Navy, we had full use of the Scout Hut which we had built in the village. We had Home Guard uniforms and told the locals that we were a Boy Scout Unit to be trained along the lines of the original Baden-Powell Army Scouts to carry messages, and this was accepted. We were careful to ensure that no-one saw any of the special equipment and our Tommy gun, pistols, and Fairbairn daggers were never exposed. We built a straw dummy for our dagger practice.

I remember my main worry was that the enemy would be able to find our OB using tracker dogs. My father trained gun dogs at home and I had seen many instances where a dog could follow the scent of a human after several hours. We had look out posts round the OB where we could pick off tracker dogs with the .22 rifle if necessary. We also planned to use rabbit as a bait with strychnine, if tracker dogs were encountered.

Broadheath Scout Hut prior to the Second World War with some of the scouts and later members of Samson Patrol painting it. Geoff Devereux is on the ladder, Rob Boaz at the bottom of the flag pole, Ron Seymour standing in front of the window and Arch Clines on the roof.
(Courtesy of Geoff Devereux)

> We amused ourselves by entering factories guarded by the Home
> Guard at night and chalking rude remarks at strategic points and
> retreating without being detected.

Geoff supplies a number of references to the weapons issued to the patrol and from subsequent discussions with other patrol members it has been possible to establish the range of weapons issued to them. The patrol was provided with a Thompson sub-machinegun for protection and several of the 50 round drum magazines were supplied for it. They had at least one, possibly two, .300 P17 rifles. The .22 rifle mentioned above was not a standard issue but a civilian rifle that had been handed in to the police in the early part of the war. Geoff remembers that it had been passed on to his father for safe-keeping. He had kept the .22 in his gun cabinet until the patrol took it over. Nevertheless

it was fitted with a silencer and telescopic sight. Apart from Geoff Devereux, who had a .32 automatic, each of the other members of the patrol were provided with a Smith and Wesson revolver. Ron Seymour remembers that they had been issued with left-handed holsters which made drawing their pistols difficult. They managed to adapt the holsters, however, although it meant wearing them on the opposite side of their belt to normal. In addition to the Fairbairn-Sykes knife, two knuckle-dusters were provided for each person and there is photographic evidence that there was at least one wooden knobkerrie available. However, what they were supposed to do with these latter weapons is not at all clear to Geoff after all these years!

Joe King and Arch Clines at Broadheath
in August 1940, toting their
Smith and Wesson revolvers
(Courtesy of Joe King)

Geoff Devereux tells us that he was not happy storing some of their 'nasties' in the OB and fairly soon after occupying it, he and the patrol buried the phosphorous grenades and Sticky Bombs in water-proof containers, probably dustbins, on the edge of the wood, near the main A44, until they were ready to use them. He often wonders what happened to them and assumes they were cleared away at the end of the war when the OB was decommissioned.

Geoff Devereux has also added more detail about their early operational training:

> My brief was for my unit to go underground in our OB as soon as the invasion occurred and to operate entirely independently thereafter. I was not to expect any contact with my superiors for at least several weeks, by which time they would try to arrange to replenish our, by that time, completely exhausted stocks of explosives and 'nasties'.

Subsequent discussion with Geoff Devereux about the apparent inconsistency between their estimated life expectancy and the need to replenish their stocks after several weeks, reveals that the patrol, if they still existed, would have made contact with the van Moppes brothers for resupply. Although Geoff has no knowledge of how this would be achieved, the need for possible resupply was clearly considered which suggests that caches of explosives and grenades existed in secure stores elsewhere in the county. Wolverton Hall may have held a stock of supplies in much the same way as Captain Sandford did at Eye Manor. Certainly Quartermaster Sergeant Dawe, who lived at Wolverton Hall, would have had responsibility for supply, but how he would have achieved this during a German occupation remains a mystery.

Geoff Devereux also recalls their targets in the event of invasion:

> Our main targets were to be night attacks on enemy laagers and to destroy as many tanks and other enemy vehicles as possible. Two of the potential vehicle laagers we had identified were Broad Green, about half a mile to the west of our OB, and Broadheath Common, about one and a half miles to the north-east. Laybys and wide road verges that could be used for vehicle parking were also noted. It is obvious too that one of our targets would have been the former railway line between Worcester and Bromyard which would have been used by the Germans to carry troops and equipment into the Midlands. It was only about half a mile to the south of the OB and could easily be reached by fording the Teme. We were to use delay equipment, where possible, to give us time to get well away from the targets. We therefore had a chart in the OB with times marked on to selected points. Having recce'd the times to each destination, this would allow us to set appropriate time pencils to give us time to get back to base, after laying the explosive charges. We had an old bicycle hidden in the wood so that one of us could ride round the area in overalls to locate possible targets. We often lay in wait outside local pubs

to listen to the gossip after closing time as we felt this might prove to be a useful source of information.

The local Army instructor referred to in connection with fitness training and unarmed combat was Peter Price, a pre-war boxer from Worcester and son of a prominent local butcher who then ran a shop in The Shambles. Peter Price trained the members of Samson Patrol at the Broadheath Scout Hut on a weekly basis but occasionally the classes were held at the Silver Street Drill Hall. Geoff Devereux also remembers some of the patrol going to the rifle range at Tyddesley Wood, near Pershore, for shooting practice and Norton Barracks for grenade practice.

The Scout Hut sadly no longer exists but it used to stand to the west of Broadheath Common and to the south of the drive to Grange Farm. Apparently in an attempt to disguise their activities as much as possible the patrol often attended their Auxiliary training sessions in scout uniform. Captain Todd also visited the Scout Hut to give the patrol instruction on the use of explosives and on one occasion is said to have amply demonstrated the relatively harmless properties of plastic explosive.

Ron Seymour recalls that the patrol also went on a number of occasions to a quarry on Bredon Hill for explosives and revolver practise. They would also visit Overbury Court, where he can remember meeting Thurston Holland-Martin, whom he thought at the time was the local commander of the Worcestershire Auxiliaries. It is interesting to find that other local Auxiliaries had the same impression.

The wrecked Samson Patrol car near Middle Lightwood Farm, Broadheath.
(Courtesy of Joe King)

Ron can also remember trying out their grenades by throwing them into the River Teme, near Bransford Bridge, and being amazed at the number of dead and stunned fish that came to the surface.

A small Morris car was provided for the patrol to use as transport by the van Moppes brothers with an ample supply of petrol coupons. This vehicle had apparently previously belonged to one of their wives. Into this all six members of the patrol would be squeezed when they wished to attend exercises elsewhere. Ron Seymour remembers that the car was originally stored at Burnhams Garage, near the Corn Market in Worcester, while John Boaz recalls that later it was kept where he lived, at Middle Lightwood Farm, Crown East. It was eventually written off when Arch Clines, who was driving, attempted to take a sharp bend too quickly near the farm and turned it over. John was one of the first on the scene and found Arch with his head through the

Ron Seymour, one of the original members of Samson Patrol, February 2001.
(Mick Wilks)

sunroof of the wrecked car. The back of the car had to be lifted in order to extricate the unfortunate driver before he was taken to the Infirmary in Worcester. Later this car was replaced by the van Moppes with a Wolseley which had to be collected from one of the garages in Farrier Street, Worcester. This may have been Wakefields but John tells us that whoever supplied the car certainly knew about the Auxiliaries. So much for secrecy!

Ron Seymour had joined the Meco Works LDV/Home Guard in May 1940 and when he was recruited to the Auxiliaries, chose to retain his Home Guard uniform and continue to attend at least some of their parades as a cover for his more clandestine role. He therefore informed the Meco Platoon Commander, Lieutenant Byrne, that he had joined this special scouting unit at Broadheath and that he would not be able to attend all of the parades. This was apparently accepted but this knowledge of the special unit by the Home Guard commander was to lead to some combined Home Guard/Auxiliary exercises being organised—see chapter 9. It was also to lead to some mild embarrassment for Ron. On one occasion, when collecting the Samson Patrol car from Burnham's Garage, he was spotted by his Meco Platoon Home Guard colleagues, who were marching by. Ron was in uniform, wearing his revolver, and the Platoon Commander promptly saluted him!

Joe King in August 2000. (Mick Wilks)

Ron was married late in 1941 and he tells us that the van Moppes provided his wife with a small .22 pistol for her own protection. This, presumably, was in case the Gestapo came looking for her should Ron have been captured or someone had informed on his special role. At this time Ron and his wife were living with his in-laws in St John's and his personal weapons, which included his Smith and Wesson and a P17 rifle were kept in the wardrobe. This was kept locked and an instruction given to his in-laws not to go into it. Interestingly Ron says he had to provide his own sheath knife; he was not issued with the Fairbairn-Sykes knife.

By late 1941, Geoff Devereux, Rob Boaz and Joe King had left Samson

John Boaz in January 2000
(Mick Wilks)

Patrol, to go into the regular forces, while Ron Seymour had been offered other reserved employment with Dowty's of Cheltenham. For a while he would return to Broadheath at weekends to train with the patrol but finally left in 1942. John Boaz, Peter King and Peter Wright were recruited in 1941 to replace these losses by the new Sergeant, Val Clines. Arch Clines left the patrol later in the war to join the Merchant Navy so that by 1944, when the final Nominal Rolls were recorded, the patrol had become quite small and comprised Val Clines (Sergeant and Patrol Leader), John Boaz, Peter King and Peter Wright. No Corporal appears to have been appointed at any stage.

One interesting sequel to Geoff Devereux's time in the Samson Patrol is that a couple of years after he left and was serving in the Grenadier Guards, he was suddenly called to Sunningdale where there was a captured Royal Tiger tank on show. 'I was asked how this German tank could be destroyed as the British/US Army had no armament which could pierce the 8 inches of armoured plate on the front. I wonder how much that journey had to do with my earlier Auxiliary experience! There almost certainly would have been a reference to it on my Service Record'.

When Ron Seymour took up his new position with the Dowty Company, then manufacturing aircraft undercarriage systems, he enquired about joining an Auxiliary patrol in that area. He was told by Captain Todd that this would not be possible because there were none. Certainly the Nominal Rolls do not have any Auxiliaries listed for Gloucestershire, which is a strange omission but, if there were, perhaps John Todd thought it would be unwise having one person with the knowledge of two patrols?

John Boaz has many memories of the later years of the Samson Patrol, including the loss of their HQ at the Scout Hut.

> I was asked by Val Clines, who was then Sergeant, if I would like to volunteer. This was about July, 1941. I was not yet 18 and it was suggested that I joined the local Home Guard, get a uniform and then transfer to the Samson Patrol on my birthday, a couple of weeks later. When I left the Home Guard, I used black enamel to paint all the brass buckles and buttons on my uniform in keeping with my new role. In fact the local Home Guard were the biggest enemy of our patrol. They were mostly First World War soldiers and all 'spit and polish'. Most Sundays, after training, we would go up to The Plough, at Broadheath, for a drink and there would be the Home Guard, who had been on parade and all polished up. We would turn up in our rubber boots and denims, and plastered in clay. They always tried to find out what we were up to but they did not find out much!

The rubber boots to which John refers were widely issued to the Auxiliaries and he describes them as really good lace-up boots which were totally waterproof. He remembers that they were still available commercially after the war but not now. These were, of course, much quieter in use than the conventional military hob-nailed boot which had been issued earlier but John tells us that, even now, as a result of his Auxiliary training, people do not hear him approaching. It is apparently all to do with putting your heels down slowly!

When the Scout Master and the more senior members of the Broadheath Scout Troop had left the village, Ron Seymour became responsible for the Scout Hut. After Ron left the village, John became the key holder. The local Home Guard, who had previously established their HQ in Broadheath Church Hall, decided that they wanted to use the Scout Hut instead and John was compelled to hand over the key.

We Auxiliaries were mad devils in those days and come the day we were to hand over the hut, we put a trip wire from the door down under the steps where we laid a booby trap in the form of a detonator. When Sergeant Taylor of the Broadheath Home Guard opened the door, the trap went off with a loud bang. Unfortunately the blast picked up some gravel that damaged the butt of his rifle which had been propped by the side of the door. There was hell to pay after that! The van Moppes had to come and smooth things over with the local Home Guard officers at Aymestry School.

After leaving the Scout Hut, we moved our HQ down to Middle Lightwood Farm, near Cotheridge. This belonged to my father and we stored all our explosives and ammunition in the cellar. If my parents had known what was stored there they would probably not have slept at night! In those days the family used to store potatoes, cider barrels and so on down there. The explosives were stored near the centre of the cellar, where the steps went down and it was dark. They were hidden under old drain pipes and corrugated iron. There were boxes and boxes of the stuff, including booby traps, trip wire and timers. We also had rolls and rolls of steel wire which was to be used to stretch across a road in order to chop off the heads of German despatch riders. Another evil device we had, in some quantity, was pencil sized, with a button at one end and a single bullet at the other. These were intended to be pushed into the pathways used by enemy sentries and when trodden on would fire the bullet through the sentry's foot. [This is the AP Switch described on pp.49 & 51] We had pull switches which were used for setting booby traps such as under lavatory seats and various length time fuses for use with explosives. I remember that one of the tasks we would have had after an invasion was to blow up enemy fuel dumps.

From time to time, officers would call on the patrol at Broadheath to check their stores of explosives and if anything was 'going off' they were advised to use it for training purposes. Such an opportunity occurred when the War Agricultural Committee asked John's father to clear and plough a 15 acre field containing a large pear tree which was dying back.

We had a box of TNT which had become damp and I asked my father if we could use the old pear tree for explosives practise. He agreed and so the patrol assembled on a Sunday morning for the exercise. We put four hefty charges under the tree which was not too far from the road. While two of the patrol went onto the road to warn any passers-by, two took cover in the ditch, while the fifth connected the fuse, activated it and ran back to the ditch. There was a sudden 'woomph' and the whole tree went up into the air and disintegrated! There was not a square yard of the field which did not have bits of tree in it. Father was not at all pleased with the result. I and the rest of the patrol spent the next week picking up bits of tree before the field could be ploughed! But that is not the end of the story, Geoff Devereux's mother lived in a cottage about a quarter of a mile away and the explosion had cracked all her ceilings. Of course she knew a bit about the patrol's activities and who had done it. We probably put too much of a charge in!

John Boaz remembers the patrol going down to the Isle of Wight in 1944, as a voluntary duty, with the van Moppes brothers.

We were all supplied with Sten guns, which were very temperamental, and we assembled at Bulmers' Cider Factory in Hereford, who were something to do with the organisation. [This is more likely to have been the Watkins Pomona Cider Works at Holmer with which 'Hughie' Hall of the Herefordshire Auxiliaries was connected]. We slept in one of the factory buildings until about 4 o'clock in the morning when we were picked up by an army lorry and transported to the Isle of Wight. Here we were accommodated in a bell-tented camp where we slept during the day and then did all-night guard duty. On one occasion we were patrolling a road, at night, with the van Moppes, when we could hear footsteps in the distance coming towards us. One of the van Moppes brothers said that we should do the job properly, get down onto the ditch and when the approaching people came alongside, he would get up and shout 'halt', at which time the rest of the patrol should be ready for action. The two shadowy figures were duly challenged and in the course of jumping out of the ditch one of the patrol unfortunately slipped and dropped the butt of his Sten onto the road. The whole magazine was uncontrollably fired off. Nobody was hurt but the result was two very frightened soldiers who had been out of the camp visiting local girls!

I had not previously seen anything like the Isle of Wight, where there were dumps of munitions all over the island in preparation for the D-Day landings. Pioneer Corps troops were loading shells all day from 6

Samson Patrol reunion, March 2001.
Left to right: Bert Davies, former Special Duties radio mechanic at Coleshill;
Geoff Devereux, the first Samson Patrol sergeant; Ron Seymour, one of the
original members of the patrol; Peter Wright and John Boaz, two of the later
members of the patrol. (Mick Wilks)

o'clock in the morning until 8 o'clock at night. I felt very sorry for the Pioneers who did not have a decent uniform between them!

John Boaz also recalls having competitions where they had to fire a single round with the Sten but he says that this was virtually impossible; he considered the earlier Tommy gun to be a lovely weapon. His Smith and Wesson proved to be useful in the harvesting season, for he would carry it on their Fordson tractor when towing the binder, stopping from time to time to pot rabbits as they came out of the corn! The Fairbairn-Sykes knife was provided with a leather sheath and he recalls that their patrol cut a slit in their trousers so that the sheath could be strapped directly to the leg. This enabled them to draw the knife more easily.

John tells us that he enjoyed his time with the Auxiliaries but is under no illusions about their role. He has no doubt that their OB would have been found by the Germans.

Joshua Patrol

Roger Smith of Commandary Farm was the first sergeant of this patrol which was formed at Crowle, but he is no longer alive. What follows is based on the memories of John Wythes and Jim Holt, apparently the only survivors at the time of writing. Roger Smith, who was already a member of the Crowle LDV/Home Guard, must have been recruited by Captain Todd too but, as he was fairly new to the village, he asked his friend John Wythes to help him recruit the remainder of the patrol. John was a fellow Home Guardsman and the son of the farmer who occupied Rectory Farm, immediately adjoining Commandary Farm, in Lower Crowle. In turn John recruited Jim Holt, who was a shooting friend and the then gardener to Captain Castle at Froxmere Court, Ivor Thomas from Crowle Green, Noel Huband, who was the son of the village shopkeeper and Jack Badger from Broughton Hackett. All were already members of the Home Guard and well known to each other. John, who knew the van Moppes very well and regularly went shooting with them in their extensive grounds at Wolverton Hall, thought that they had been instrumental in arranging the transfer of the patrol members from the Home Guard to the Auxiliaries. Jim Holt remembers that the patrol continued to attend Home Guard parades in uniform to avoid drawing undue attention to themselves from the locals. Nevertheless, as elsewhere the local Home Guard became rivals of the patrol, although they apparently did not find their OB.

The patrol headquarters, when the Operational Base was not used, was either at Roger Smith's house at Commandary Farm or alternatively at Wolverton Hall. The patrol usually met on a weekly basis for instruction and training, some of which was at Coleshill. Local training was usually at Commandary Farm, where they would receive lectures or further training in unarmed combat from Peter Price. Nocturnal fieldcraft and some explosives training was undertaken in the fields belonging to Roger Smith, to the east of Commandary Farm and alongside Bow Brook. Jim Holt explained that 'this land was well away from the road and the prying eyes of the villagers. As part of our training we used to roll small quantities of PE into a ball and throw it into Bow Brook to kill fish for the pot!' Apparently chubb, trout and roach were obtained in this way. Members of John Wythes' family can recall hearing stories of night-time explosions around the village being attributed to the German bombers that used to regularly over fly Worcestershire!

Some training was received at the Drill Hall in Silver Street, Worcester, including unarmed combat from Peter Price and lectures. On these occasions, the patrol would cycle to and from Crowle, leaving their bikes at The Plough Inn, in Lowesmoor. Other training was at Wolverton Hall including night patrols and rifle shooting. Later, competitions were held there with the other Worcestershire patrols. At Wolverton Hall, Jim Holt recalled, the van Moppes used to entertain the Auxiliaries after the exercises with wonderfully cooked food! Joshua Patrol also went to Overbury to use the quarry for explosives training and revolver firing practice, organised by Thurston Holland-Martin. Again the patrol was entertained afterwards in Overbury Court and Jim remembered splendid meals being provided by the Holland-Martin family. On one occasion Roger Smith apparently embarrassed himself by referring, in a 'thank you' speech, to the wonderfully cooked chicken, only to be told by the hosts that it was rabbit!

Joshua Patrol had two Operational Bases. Their first one was constructed to the east of Crowle village, occupying woodland, then owned by the Croome Estate and overlooking Upton Snodsbury. A separate underground munitions store was provided and apparently sited some distance away. From this information it is possible to deduce that the primary role of the patrol would have been to harass German troops using the main A422 approach to Worcester from the east. It is also likely that the main north-south railway line from Birmingham to Cheltenham, which passes by Crowle a mile to the west, would have been on their list of potential targets. To this list could be added Spetchley Court, which would have had an obvious attraction as a headquarters for German occupation forces.

This first OB was constructed by Royal Engineers but was abandoned almost immediately because it flooded, and was replaced by another structure built in the woods, then owned by Captain Castle, on the north-west side of the village. This second site provides good views over the intervening flat land

Jim Holt (left) and former Sergeant John Wythes, both of Joshua Patrol, June 2000. (Mick Wilks)

between Crowle and Worcester, and towards Droitwich. Little remains of the first OB, where only a large hole caused by the collapsed main chamber can be seen, and the munitions store has not yet been found, but the second OB is more complete. Although this has also recently collapsed it is possible to see that it is of the same form as that which still exists at Alfrick, with vertical brick access shaft, main chamber and a munitions store off to one side of the access shaft. The sewer pipe escape tunnel is still apparent and is now used by badgers as a sett.

Both John and Jim recalled the patrol staying in the second OB for weekends or longer and that the experience was reasonably comfortable. Lighting was by hurricane lamp and John could remember them being careful when cooking, to avoid fumes issuing from the ventilators. Jim told us that on one occasion during a nightime exercise to set trip wires and detonators around the OB, they were discovered by a person who lived close by. He was out looking for his pigs, which had wandered into the woods and, as a consequence of seeing their OB entrance, he was immediately sworn to secrecy. He was also told that should there be an invasion he would have to join the patrol in the OB.

This OB was provided with a telephone, which was connected to another handset in a hidden observation post set up in a large tree some distance away. Apparently these telephones were also connected to a line back to the village, presumably to Roger Smith. However the primary purpose of the system was to enable the outside observer to speak to the patrol leader in the OB and inform him of approaching enemy patrols and so enable an escape, or the presence of convoys and potential targets to be notified.

Since their OB was damp, their arms, ammunition and explosives were stored in the fruit room at Froxmere Court. This adjoined Jim Holt's cottage alongside the walled garden and could only be accessed through the garden tool store. Jim had the key to the fruit room and so became responsible for the munitions. He was issued with the patrol's .22 rifle and often used it on the estate for shooting rabbits. On other occasions the whole patrol used this rifle for target practice. Jim became very proficient with this weapon and reached the finals of a national shooting competition just as the Auxiliaries were stood down and the competition at Coleshill was cancelled.

Other weapons issued to Joshua Patrol included a number of other rifles, probably the .300 American made P17. There was also a Thompson submachinegun which was later replaced by a Sten. Each patrol member had the Fairbairn-Sykes knife, which, like the Samson Patrol members, was worn inside the trouser leg, and the Smith and Wesson .38 revolver. Roger Smith had a smaller calibre revolver than the rest of the patrol, probably a .32, and Jim Holt remembered an occasion when he almost shot himself in the leg with it. Apparently the patrol were on an exercise near Bow Wood and Roger Smith was fingering the trigger of his revolver, which was still holstered and strapped to his belt, when it went off. The bullet missed his leg by a fraction and went into the ground by his foot!

At the end of the war a Regular Army officer and corporal came to collect up the arms and explosives and when the store was opened up much of the equipment had deteriorated due to damp and had to be destroyed. This included some of the weapons, which had badly rusted. Their destruction was achieved by heaping up both weapons and explosives in a nearby field and detonating them.

This patrol apparently did not go to the Isle of Wight for guard duty.

David Patrol

It is difficult to deduce which patrol was formed next but the existence of a small grassed airfield at Tilesford must have attracted John Todd's attention. The possibility of this being used by transport aircraft of occupying German forces led him to recruit a patrol nearby at an early stage. Alec Fernihough, a farmer from Radford, was chosen to lead the patrol, which was given the code name 'David'. Alec Fernihough was a pre-war boxer of some repute and his ability to look after himself were ideal credentials for a patrol sergeant. The rest of the patrol comprised Harry and Colin Curnock, Tom Harwood, Harold Plain, Ernie Shervington and Harold Wilkins, all from the farming community of the Abbots Lench, Abbots Morton and Radford area.

At the time of writing, the late Colin Curnock, Tom Harwood and Harold Wilkins helped us to establish the background to David Patrol. All members of the patrol were approached on an individual basis by Alec Fernihough and transferred from the Home Guard because the Auxiliaries promised a much more interesting and exciting prospect. Although the members of the David Patrol were well known to their former colleagues in the Home Guard and their training activities were also apparent, their OB location remained secret throughout the war. It was not unusual for the patrol to be marching in one direction on a Sunday morning, perhaps to practise shooting at a local quarry, and the Home Guard to be marching in the opposite direction on one of their exercises. The secrecy which is supposed to have surrounded the activities of the Auxiliaries was perhaps not as close as it might have been in the rural areas! Knowledge of members of other patrols, particularly since the majority were

Colin Curnock, formerly of David Patrol, December 1999. (Mick Wilks)

recruited from the close-knit Worcestershire farming community also seems to have been widespread.

The headquarters for the patrol was at Alec Fernihough's house at Grove Farm, where the members would meet on Sunday mornings to discuss their training schemes or to practise using their weapons and explosives. For this latter purpose the patrol used Kington Break, a former quarry, to the west of Grove Farm. Alec Fernihough's son, John, who still farms from the family home, remembers the noise of firing and explosions on Sundays sounding as though the German invasion had taken place!

Transport for the patrol was provided either by Alec Fernihough, who would use his own car, or by Harry Curnock, who also had a vehicle. Contact was maintained with the van Moppes by Alec Fernihough visiting Wolverton Hall on the first Monday of each month, taking with him another member of the patrol. This was often Tom Harwood. There was apparently no telephone provided at the OB.

All surviving members of David Patrol were clear about their operational role. This was to observe Pershore Airfield and after invasion, to attack and destroy any German aircraft which may be using it. By the middle of 1940, this former private flying field, near Tilesford Farm was being expanded to become a fully developed RAF Bomber Command Operational Training Unit airfield with the conventional concrete runways and hangars—well situated for use by German aircraft bringing in reinforcements and supplies for attacks against the important munitions producing areas of Birmingham, Coventry and the Black Country once the area was occupied.

To facilitate their role, the patrol was provided with an Operational Base about two miles to the east of the airfield, at the highest point of a wooded ridgeline. From here the patrol would have had a good view of the airfield, be able to assess where enemy aircraft were parked and work on their plans for night attacks against them. Their OB was apparently not of the usual metal elephant shelter construction but was a more substantial brick structure, and built by Espleys of Evesham, rather than Royal Engineers. Nevertheless it had the conventional vertical shaft entrance, which was heavily camouflaged, and an escape tunnel. To avoid disturbing the very good camouflage of the entrance shaft the patrol members tended to use the escape tunnel as their usual means of access and egress on their visits to the OB. The main shaft was used primarily to reprovision the OB, when food and equipment would be lowered down the shaft or lifted out when necessary. The entrance to the OB was apparently marked by a large oak tree, which must have helped them to locate it in the dark. Visits by the patrol to the OB were about once a fortnight when they would sometimes stay overnight, but never longer. This OB survived until about two years ago when it appears to have been demolished as part of a plan to develop the woods as a competition trap shooting ground.

The arms and explosives store for David Patrol was beneath the granary store steps at Grove Farm, Radford. These can be seen to the right and beyond the pony and rider. The steps have since been demolished. (Courtesy of John Fernihough)

Because of damp problems in the OB the patrol's munitions were stored in a secure space under lock and key below the stone steps leading up to the grain store at Grove Farm. Colin Curnock remembered that each member of the patrol was issued with a Smith and Wesson revolver for personal protection and that he also had a brand new .22 rifle with which he had won a shooting competition at Lower Wolverton. Colin had handled guns for most of his life and it is likely that his skill had him marked out as the patrol sniper. Tom Harwood remembers having an FS knife and travelling to Hereford for training by Regular Army officers, where there was an assault course, he thought somewhere near a cider factory. This was almost certainly the Watkins Pomona Works at Holmer. He also remembers that the patrol had an automatic weapon, possibly a Sten, on which they practised firing in either single or automatic modes. The initial training for the patrol was at Coleshill. Some of the explosives issued to the patrol were later used to remove tree stumps in the Lenches area. Indeed one member of the patrol is reputed to have made a business of removing trees for local farmers, using the David Patrol explosives—and charging for it!

David Patrol did not go to the Isle of Wight for guard duties.

Jehu Patrol

Doctor Tony Barling, then a young medical student, joined the LDV in May 1940 at Knightwick in Worcestershire, the nearest unit to his parents' home at Alfrick Court. The Commanding Officer of this unit was Doctor Roger Clarke, the local GP, and some time after the LDV had been formed he asked for volunteers for an unspecified job. The attraction of doing something with a frisson of danger and excitement appealed to Tony Barling and, having put his name forward, was visited by Captain Todd. After introducing himself, John Todd proceeded to drop a package of plastic explosive on the floor, his usual technique for testing the nerves of the prospective Auxilier and at the same time demonstrating the relative ease of handling this powerful explosive. Following the usual swearing in process, Tony Barling was told what his new role was to be and asked to pick the rest of his patrol. From his fellow LDVs he chose John Barker, Chris Bullock, George Dalley, Bill Jauncey, Reg Mason and Bill Plaskett, all local lads who knew the lie of the land.

The code name 'Jehu' was chosen by the van Moppes for the patrol because this biblical character apparently drove his chariot furiously—in those days Tony Barling drove a TT Replica chain drive Fraser-Nash which other Auxiliaries can recall being driven very rapidly. In 1940, Tony Barling would work at his medical studies in Birmingham during the week, returning to Alfrick for the weekends to spend time with his patrol. Petrol coupons for two gallons of petrol were supplied to him which was just about enough to make the return journey to Birmingham.

Although most of the venues for the patrol training in the early

Dr Tony Barling, former Sergeant of Jehu Patrol, January 2000.
(Mick Wilks)

days have been lost in the mists of time, Tony Barling can remember going to Wolverton Hall for night patrols. However, he can recall in some detail making up packages of plastic explosive, putting in two time pencils to make sure they went off and binding the completed packages with sticky tape. He also used Bickford fuse, which burned at 2 feet a second and Instantaneous fuse, the latter presumably for booby trap work. The patrol practised with Sticky Bombs against an old traction engine, which in retrospect he thought was a shame. Tony Barling thought the Sticky Bomb was a wonderful weapon, as long as it did not stick to your clothes! Another weapon which impressed him was the Thompson sub-machinegun which he remembers coming in a beautiful wooden box. He practised firing this at Alfrick Court against one of the brick walls, a wall subsequently repaired with concrete blocks. Tony Barling was especially proud of the Thompson because he had been supplied with one before the Commandos, his older brother being a Major in that unit.

Only part of the patrol appear to have gone to Coleshill for training. John

Barker, for example, who was in the patrol for just a few months before transferring to the Transport Platoon of the Worcester City Home Guard, can only remember crawling around the local countryside at night as his training. Chris Bullock can recall going to a quarry near Evesham for explosives and revolver shooting practise, this probably being the quarry on Bredon Hill used by other patrols. Tony Barling tells us that Thurston Holland-Martin was one of the senior organisers of the Auxiliaries in Worcestershire and not just the Sergeant of the Overbury Patrol. 'Gug' or Edmund van Moppes, the younger of the two brothers, was Dr Barling's immediate senior officer and seemed a very nice, easy going sort of person.

The remains of Jehu Patrol's first Operational Base at Alfrick. The wartime strengthening brickwork to support the floor of the munitions store can still be seen in the back wall. (Mick Wilks)

At the outset, the primary role of Jehu Patrol was to harass

Bernard Lowry climbing down the entrance shaft of the Jehu Patrol's second OB on a wet day in 1999. (Mick Wilks)

the German forces passing through their operational area, although Tony Barling thought they would also have had an observation role, watching for German troops using the main A44 and the railway line between Leominster and Worcester. The observation role is very likely because his sister, Elizabeth Barling, was recruited as a courier for the patrol, her role being to pick up messages left by her brother in an old metal teapot which was placed in a hedgerow not far from their OB. These were to be taken to the van Moppes, who would presumably then relay the content of these to the Regular forces or other Auxiliary patrols. It is also feasible that the patrol would have had an ambush role, for they were trained in the use of the Sticky Bomb and also had a stock of AW Bombs. The gap through the hills at Knightwick, which in this area form a substantial barrier to troop movements from the west heading towards Worcester, would be a good position for ambuscades. Tony Barling also thought the patrol would, if necessary, have destroyed the bridge over the Teme at Knightwick, to delay the Germans.

Jehu Patrol had two OBs, the first being a temporary facility in a small, above ground, farm building, which had been adapted by Royal Engineers. A very strong concrete floor was inserted into the top of the building so that their arms and explosives could be stored at first floor level. This building has been largely demolished but sufficient remains for the wartime brickwork strengthening that carried this heavy floor, to be apparent. This OB is now in an open position, but during the war was in part of the extensive woodlands to the north-west of Alfrick village. Once their underground OB had been completed a short distance away, on the west side of the hills, the original facility became simply a secure store for their munitions. Should an invasion occur, then they would have been moved to the main underground base.

Tony Barling remembers that the AW Bombs started to 'go off' after a while and that the patrol buried these in the woodland, close to their original OB. For this purpose his father's metal campaign trunk was used to incarcerate them. Apparently his father was not pleased to give up his trunk, but was told that his country needed it!

The munitions store of the Jehu Patrol's second OB, with the corrugated Anderson shelter sections clearly seen. (Mick Wilks)

Jehu Patrol's underground OB is still largely intact, and has been described on pp.33-34. Apparently a number of the Alfrick locals observed the Royal Engineers taking materials to the site of the underground OB, knowledge that would have been a potential threat to the security of the patrol, had there been an invasion.

Jehu Patrol seems to have had an unusually large number of personnel changes during its early life. John Barker left after only a matter of months and Chris Bullock left quite early on to join the RAF. Bill Jauncey and Reg Mason also left the patrol after a short time and one of the replacements was Horace Phillips who transferred from the Suckley Home Guard in early 1941. He went to the OB only twice during the short time he was a member of the patrol, and could not find it on either occasion because it was so well camouflaged—he had to have another member of the patrol to show him where it was. He can recall, however, that the air intake for the OB was through a hole in the butt of a tree. Horace went to Coleshill for training, travelling down with Bill Plaskett in an Army staff car, and remembers that Captain Todd had to secure his release from the Meco works. This was the winter and Horace can remember arriving at Coleshill absolutely frozen, but was greeted with the best cup of tea he can recall having during the wartime. He also remembers the stables being particularly cold to sleep in.

On their return to Alfrick, local training included visits to the quarry at Overbury for grenade and revolver practise, and yet more instruction on unarmed combat. The patrol travelled to Overbury in cars, Horace using his own Morris Eight for which he had a 'G' licence (a licence issued to owners on Government business) and petrol coupons. Another local exercise, in the woods at Alfrick, involved setting trip wires and blowing up trees. During training the patrol would wear their denims and the normal field service cap.

Horace Phillips left the Auxiliaries in July 1942 and handed in his revolver to Tony Barling's father at Alfrick Court. On moving to Leigh, Horace joined the Home Guard again and became part of the Leigh Platoon medical team for which he had to go to Malvern to train.

Jim Griffin joined the patrol in early 1942, after some of the others had left. Dr Barling was still the sergeant and Jim can remember patrol meetings being held around the table at Alfrick Court. Jim remained in the patrol until stand-down in 1944 and he has a number of

Horace Phillips of Alfrick, an early member of Jehu Patrol, April 2001. (Mick Wilks)

memories of the patrol's later years. For local weapons training, including rifle shooting, Jim can remember going to Bredon Hill, presumably the quarry on the Overbury estate recalled by others. However, some grenade practise was carried out in the fields to the west of Ravenhills Wood. Other training took place at Wolverton Hall on Sunday mornings. After training at Wolverton Hall, the patrol would stop at the Berkeley Arms, at Egdon, for refreshment.

Jim Griffin, former member of Jehu Patrol, April 2001. (Mick Wilks)

Jim also remembers that the patrol had some quantity of plastic explosive and Nobels 808. He recalls with some pleasure one occasion of its use. Captain Sandford was testing the individual members of the patrol on how to make up their explosive charges, for which it was necessary to tie a reef knot in the detonating cord. The then sergeant, who shall remain nameless, managed to tie a granny knot and had his 'leg pulled' as a result.

Of the weapons, Jim can remember that George Dalley later had a Sten gun, while he himself was quite successful with the patrol's .22 rifle, coming sixth in the county shooting competition. Like Jim Holt of Joshua Patrol, he was due to go down to Coleshill for the final competition, when the Auxiliaries were stood down.

During 1942, members of the patrol were asked if they would like to volunteer for duty in Norway, which confirms what Jim Thornton of Jacob Patrol at Bromyard said, but apparently no-one did.

Tony Barling left the patrol to join the Parachute Regiment sometime after 1942. Apparently he felt that as his elder brother was a Major in the Commandos and had a green beret, he wanted to have a red one! He became a Medical Officer in the regiment, which was to lead him to Arnhem and capture, spending the rest of the war in a German prisoner of war camp. Sergeant Dawe from Wolverton Hall ran Jehu Patrol for a short time, until George Dalley was made up to Sergeant. George Dalley had been in the Regular Army before the war and then worked for the War Agricultural Committee in Worcestershire. It is likely that he recruited Arthur Allen and Pete Bussey to the patrol since they worked for the same organisation. Arthur Allen became the patrol corporal. Joe Poole from Broadheath joined the patrol in 1944, almost at the end of its existence.

Some time after Doctor Barling left the patrol, a telephone was installed in the Operational Base and the patrol members dug a shallow trench along the woodland ride for the cable to an Observation Post overlooking the railway. The trench was refilled and replanted to disguise the presence of the cable, which had been covered with a bituminous outer covering and required no additional protection from the damp earth. The OP was located under a yew tree and the dugout was boarded over and the soil spread on top to provide both shelter and camouflage. A second telephone was to be installed there, when the OP was in use, for the observer to report back to the OB. From the OP the observer would have watched for the passage of trains between Leominster and Worcester and Jim confirms that the primary role of the patrol, by the time he had joined, was to have disrupted German troop movements on this railway. The railway no longer exists but there were two viaducts in the vicinity which could have been destroyed with explosives to achieve that aim.

The patrol went to the Isle of Wight for a fortnight at around the time of the D-Day landings and travelled down by Army lorry. They were billeted in the warden's house next to Albany Barracks and carried out night patrols while there. The greatest excitement was a Doodlebug (V1) exploding three or four hundred yards away.

The Claines Patrol

The biblical code name for the patrol is not remembered. However, the patrol was eventually to be led by Dick Philips, a farmer's son from Claines. He had joined the local platoon of the LDV/Home Guard and sometime afterwards was approached by Gerald Rowe of Blanquettes Avenue, Worcester, about joining the Auxiliaries. They had been at the Worcester King's School together and were close friends. Gerald Rowe had in turn been approached by Alan Dorrell, another ex-King's School boy and a friend of the van Moppes. Alan Dorrell was in the RAF at the time and was unfortunately killed quite early in the war. Captain Todd does not appear to have been involved in the process of recruiting this patrol. Dick Philips and Gerald Rowe recruited the remaining members— George Graham, Andrew Green, Hubert Jackson, Vincent Poland and Horace Roberts, all from the Ombersley area.

Vincent Poland, a Scotsman, was employed as a handyman/gardener by Lewis van Moppes, at his Ombersley home, and was probably a personal bodyguard, the handyman/gardener job being simply a cover for this more sinister function.

Horace Roberts ran Dunhampton garage and provided the transport for the patrol, an Austin 12, which was apparently driven flat out everywhere, perhaps reflecting his pre-war career in motorsport. The remainder of the patrol was largely made up with the sons of farmers.

The patrol were very quickly supplied with arms and explosives, including the new plastic explosive.

At some stage the patrol was told that it was no longer acceptable to have two men running it and that it would be necessary to choose a Sergeant. This was apparently done democratically, and Dick Philips was chosen, but this did not please Gerald Rowe who subsequently left the Auxiliaries. Vincent Poland became the patrol's Corporal.

Dick Philips, former Sergeant of the Claines Patrol, Autumn 1999. (Mick Wilks)

Initial training was carried out at Coleshill, while local practise with explosives usually involved blowing tree stumps on the various farms where the patrol members lived. TNT was used for this work, although Dick Philips considered that plastic was a far safer explosive. Some local training, including grenade throwing, was also conducted on Andrew Green's farm, where an RAF bombing decoy site was located. Their armoury included revolvers, P17 rifles and a Browning Automatic Rifle (BAR).

Although the precise function of the patrol has been forgotten now, Dick Philips tells us that their main purpose was to sabotage German installations. He points out that although the patrol members had been trained to kill, they were to avoid confrontation and the risk of being killed themselves. Their OB was located near Porter's Mill, to the north of Fernhill Heath, in a small woodland belonging to Dick Philips's father. From this siting it is possible to predict the likely objectives for the patrol after occupation of the area by German forces. First would be the airfield at Perdiswell, less than two miles to the south of their OB. High on the list of objectives for attention by the patrol would also be the large houses in the area, which would be attractive as billets for the occupying forces. These include Hindlip Hall, now West Mercia Police Headquarters, Ombersley Court, Bevere House and Bevere Manor. The latter pair of properties had already been selected by the British government as accommodation for themselves, should an invasion occur and London been lost, whilst an article in the *Sunday Mercury* during the 1970s indeed suggested that Ombersley Court had been earmarked as an SS headquarters. Other potential targets for the patrol would be the Royal Signals wireless establishment at Droitwich and the Royal Ordnance Factory at Blackpole, both being useful facilities to be occupied and reused by the Germans. Add in the ambush of convoys along the A38 and disrupting rail traffic on the line through Fernhill Heath, and the Claines Patrol could have been very busy!

The OB has gone now, filled in by Dick Philips himself about 20 years ago, when one of their bullock calves disappeared and was found some weeks later in the collapsed remains of the structure. The OB was a standard elephant shelter, with vertical shaft entrance and a short sewer pipe escape tunnel. There was apparently space within the OB for five people to sit down. A number of people have told us that they found this hide when, as children, they were exploring this canalside wood.

The explosives and ammunition for the patrol were kept initially in an unused building at Linacres Farm. Had there been an emergency they would have been quickly moved to the OB. Later the munitions were moved to Church Farm, Claines, from where they were picked up by the Army at the end of the war. Dick Philips recalls that some of their incendiary devices started to deteriorate and had to be removed earlier.

One of the problems suffered by this patrol was that a lot of people thought that the members of it were doing nothing for the war effort and of course because of their oath of secrecy were unable to defend themselves against this criticism. This still rankles and Dick Philips, who is the sole survivor of his patrol feels that the ex-Auxiliaries should have some recognition, not only for what they did in the way of training but what they were prepared to do, had there been an invasion.

This patrol did not go to the Isle of Wight for guard duty.

The Overbury Patrol

Again the biblical code name for this patrol has not been identified and other details of this patrol have been difficult to establish. Fortunately, the late Basil

Left: Sergeant Basil Tadman of the Overbury Patrol, late in the Second World War. (Courtesy of the late Basil Tadman).
Above: Basil Tadman in May 2000 with his AW Bomb case, retained postwar as a 'useful box', still with its enamelled metal plate and handling notes.
(Mick Wilks)

Tadman, the Patrol Sergeant for the latter part of the war and the sole survivor, contacted us as a result of an article in the *Malvern Gazette* about our research. This was only a short while before he died but he was able to provide us with some of the background to the patrol.

Like most of the other Auxiliaries in Worcestershire, the Overbury patrol transferred from the LDV/Home Guard and it is interesting to compare their method of recruitment with the other patrols in the county. The patrol members were all estate workers on the Overbury Court Estate and were inducted into the LDV, with the rest of their male colleagues from the estate, *en masse*, by being assembled on the village cricket field by the Holland-Martin family who were then the estate owners. Basil Tadman remembered that sometime afterwards, some of the men from the Home Guard were summoned to the library at Overbury Court by Thurston Holland-Martin and introduced to Captain Lloyd Bucknall who replaced Captain Sandford as the Intelligence Officer for both Herefordshire and Worcestershire. He swore them to secrecy and explained their new role to them. Since Captain Bucknall did not become an IO until 1943, the timing is difficult to understand. The Auxiliary personnel lists held by the Public Record Office indicate that the patrol existed in 1942, so perhaps Captain Bucknall was an assistant to John Todd and Christopher Sandford before he became the IO.

Whatever the date of their formation, Thurston Holland-Martin became the first patrol sergeant, the other members of the patrol being Jack Hall, Charlie Morris, 'Packy' Packwood, Basil Tadman and Reg Wilkinson. Basil was the farm manager of the estate and Reg Wilkinson the gamekeeper. Charlie Morris came from Dumbleton and was the estate plumber. He was later to suffer a motorcycle accident while returning to Dumbleton from Auxiliary training at Overbury, and took no further part in the patrol's activities. His place in the patrol was taken by Edmund Atkins.

Unlike elsewhere, where Royal Engineers were employed, the OB at Overbury was constructed by the estate staff, who provided both the expertise and the materials for building the underground structure. The OB apparently still exists in woodland on the south side of Bredon Hill, but Basil Tadman's memory of it indicates it was of the usual corrugated style with a short escape tunnel. The entrance cover incorporated a tree stump. The tower on the top of the hill was used by the patrol as their Observation Post, even though the Germans would also be likely to exploit its use for this purpose. The OB was apparently not provided with telephone communication with this observation post, as if the Germans were to use it, they would have quickly followed the cable back to the OB.

The explosives were stored at the OB, which suggests that it was dryer than OBs elsewhere. Basil could remember that the patrol were supplied PE, Nobels 808, Cordtex, time pencils, Sticky Bombs and No. 36 grenades. He had kept, because it was such a useful box, an AW Bomb case, so clearly the patrol were also supplied with these incendiary devices to be used for attacking enemy tanks. The Overbury patrol did not receive automatic weapons or knives, only revolvers. Captain Bucknall apparently supplied the munitions to the patrol.

Initial training for the whole patrol was undertaken at Coleshill, whilst local training was carried out on Bredon Hill or at the van Moppes' home at Wolverton Hall, where they would meet other patrols for night exercises. Besides the van Moppes, whom he knew as the Group Leaders of the Auxiliaries, he also knew Alec Fernihough, Dick Philips, Roger Smith and John Wythes, although primarily as fellow members of the National Farmers Union. He also knew Dr Barling as an Auxiliary but none of the other patrol members or of course their OB locations. Local explosives and grenade training as well as revolver practise for the patrol was carried out in an old quarry to the east of Sundial Farm on Bredon Hill, the training facility used by other patrols. Basil could not remember seeing them use it, perhaps to prevent too much collusion between the members of each patrol?

The night exercises on Bredon Hill for the Overbury patrol extended to about 5 miles, which suggests that their operational role was to be primarily within the vicinity of the hill, had there been an invasion. Although Basil Tadman could not remember their precise role, three potential targets for the patrol suggest themselves: Overbury Court itself, which would have potential as a German occupation forces HQ, Ashchurch RAOC storage depot, which would almost certainly have been reused by the Germans, and the top of Bredon Hill would then, as now, have had potential for radio signals use. To this list could be added the potential for ambushes on enemy troops using the twisting roads around the hill as well as the railway between Evesham and Tewkesbury, which used to pass close by the south side of the hill. In addition to providing the normal passenger and freight services for the area, this line also served the Ashchurch Depot.

The lists of Auxiliary personnel, held by the Public Record Office, indicate that Thurston Holland-Martin left the patrol some time after 1942. At this point Basil Tadman became the Patrol Sergeant and Jack Hall became the Corporal. In 1944, the patrol went to the Isle of Wight to carry out guard duties near Cowes. For this, the patrol did not assemble at Hereford, like the other local patrols, but made their own way in private vehicles.

Other patrols in Worcestershire?

The sites of a number of underground structures, which bear all the hallmarks of being operational bases, have come to light in Worcestershire, and suggest that there may have been other groups formed to carry out sabotage work in this area.

The Group Leaders, Sergeants and some of the Auxiliaries of the Worcestershire patrols at Wolverton Hall in 1944.
Left to right:
Back row: *Jack Badger (Joshua Patrol), Hubert Jackson (Claines Patrol), Andrew Green (Claines Patrol), John Hartwright (Joshua Patrol), 'Packy' Packwood (Overbury Patrol), Cpl Arthur Allen (Jehu Patrol), Harold Wilkins (David Patrol).*
Third row: *Tom Harwood (David Patrol), Colin Curnock (David Patrol), Jim Holt (Joshua Patrol), Horace Roberts (Claines Patrol), Jim Griffin (Jehu Patrol), Bill Plaskett (Jehu Patrol), Pete Bussey (Jehu Patrol), Reg Wilkinson (Overbury Patrol).*
Second Row: *Sgt John Wythes (Joshua Patrol), Sgt T.C. Dawe (Quartermaster Sgt, Wolverton Hall), Sgt Basil Tadman (Overbury Patrol), Sgt Val Clines (Samson Patrol), Lt Edmund van Moppes (Group Leader), Capt Lewis van Moppes (Group Leader), Lt Roger Smith (Group Leader), Sgt Dick Philips (Claines Patrol), Sgt Alec Fernihough (David Patrol), Sgt George Dalley (Jehu Patrol).*
Front Row: *Noel Huband (Joshua Patrol), Ernie Shervington (David Patrol), Harold Plain (David Patrol), Cpl Harry Curnock (David Patrol), Cpl Vincent Poland (Claines Patrol), Cpl Ivor Thomas (Joshua Patrol).*
(Courtesy of Colin Curnock)

One such structure exists at the north end of the Abberley Hills and is well located to observe and interfere with enemy columns using the main A443, Ludlow to Worcester road. This structure is of brick and concrete, has the usual vertical shaft entrance and an escape route from the other end. Although it is said to be an air raid shelter, it is possible that the Home Guard company commander at Abberley, Major Ashton, may have organised his own stay behind patrol of Home Guardsmen to use this facility and keep a watch on this pass through the hills. No documentary evidence has come to light that would support this contention, but the constructional similarity to an Auxiliary OB suggests that it was part of an official scheme.

An OB-like structure was discovered during wartime by the local boy scouts in Powick. Only a hollow remains where this structure once was, in the top of the wooded ridge at Ham Hill, but the description given to the authors fits that of an Auxiliary OB exactly—vertical shaft entrance, camouflaged with a lid containing a tray of earth with grass and other plants. Two interconnected underground chambers were provided, with an escape tunnel at the far end. Ventilation to the structure was via a pipe into the nearby hedge where it was hidden from view. Its location would have enabled the observation of enemy troop movements into Worcester from the west. There is some some evidence that this OB was for use by a Home Guard unit based at Boughton Park Golf Club House.

Another OB was constructed in the yard at Old Northwick Farm, which was then on the north-western edge of the built-up area of Worcester. Since the war the farmhouse and yard have been surrounded by new development. This was one of two OBs constructed by a Worcester builder, the other was at Ladywood, near Droitwich. As far as we know, nothing remains of these two OBs but they are remembered by a former employee of the building firm, who, like his former work colleagues, was sworn to secrecy and does not wish to divulge his name. He apparently visited the OB at Old Northwick Farm, after it was completed, to find it fully provisioned with armaments. The entrance to the underground structure here was disguised with a Gas Board manhole cover. Who were these OBs to be used by? The ones at Old Northwick Farm and Ladywood would seem to duplicate the function of that built for Dick Philips's patrol, but he has no knowledge of them. It is known that Worcester was to be heavily defended against enemy invasion forces as an 'Anti-Tank Island', the extensive defences being manned primarily by the 1st Worcestershire (Worcester) Battalion Home Guard, but did they too form stay behind patrols to carry out acts of sabotage against the occupying enemy forces? Gerry Tysoe, a former Home Guard Lieutenant, recalled that a grenade store was established in the north of the city which may have been the facility at Old Northwick Farm. This information and that relating to the Powick OB does suggest the local Home Guard may have intended to have formed such patrols but no substantive evidence has come forward for this concept.

Other OB-like structures have been reported to us in the Wythall and Hartlebury Common areas but again no evidence has come forward to link these with clandestine organisations.

CHAPTER 9
Exercises, Competitions and Demonstrations

As a test of efficiency and form of training as close to operational conditions as possible, a number of the Auxiliary patrols in the two counties were pitted against the local Home Guard, either as part of an organised scheme or informally. In chapter 8 it has already been noted how the Broadheath patrol, when led by Geoff Devereux, entered local factories guarded by their Home Guard colleagues and left rude messages chalked on machinery for them to find in the morning.

Ron Seymour, who, as has also been noted, had told his Meco Home Guard platoon commander of his specialist role with the 'Broadheath Scouts', was also asked by him to test the efficiency of the factory night guard as a solo exercise. Ron started by reconnoitring possible approaches on the previous day. In an attempt to disguise his intentions while walking around the factory buildings, he discussed the latest football results with his brother, who joined him for this part of the exercise. At the same time he was noting the Home Guard patrolling routes and timing. That night he blacked himself up with burnt cork and entered the factory site by crawling along the nearby railway embankment and down a siding into the site, a route which he had decided would give him the best chance of success. Ron had earlier constructed a dummy bomb from a tin wrapped in brown paper and marked 'bomb' and once inside he planted this in the boiler room without being spotted. He then left the premises the same way as he had come in. Having achieved his objective he thought he had better tell somebody since he could envisage a panic when the 'bomb' was eventually discovered. Ron therefore returned more obviously through the main gate and reported what he had done to the guard room.

Later, Samson Patrol, then led by Val Clines, was invited to join a Home Guard exercise involving the bridge on the A44 over Laugherne Brook, on the western outskirts of St John's, Worcester. This was again organised by the Meco Home Guard commander. Ron Seymour recalls that this was a night exercise and their task was to place dummy explosive charges under the bridge which, with its attendant road block, was guarded by his Home Guard colleagues from the Meco factory. The patrol decided to approach the bridge from the Crown East direction and across the fields to the south of the bridge. On this occasion, however, the Home Guard spotted the Auxiliaries when they were quite close to the bridge and they were 'captured'.

John Wythes remembers that the Joshua Patrol were set a similar task for a bridge near them, but they were more successful and achieved their objective without being spotted. These exercises are interesting because they imply that part of the function of Auxiliary patrols would have been to destroy bridges and so disrupt enemy convoys. Les Moore, a former Home Guardsman, from Longley Green, also remembers a combined exercise involving Jehu patrol, when the Auxiliaries were wearing a blue flash to distinguish them from their more conventional Home Guard colleagues. In this case the bridge at Knightwick is likely to have been the target.

Another exercise remembered by John Boaz involved the combined Samson and Jehu patrols and the Knightwick Home Guard. Here the Auxiliaries were to be attacked in one of the wooded hills in the Alfrick area and to protect themselves numerous trip wires and explosives were set amongst the trees. During the attack by the Home Guard, a number of the trips were activated, one fetching the top out of a tree when the explosive went off. Despite their attempts at defence the Auxiliaries were 'captured'.

An exercise, recalled by Colin Curnock, involved David Patrol having to set dummy charges under the Ledbury Railway viaduct, again guarded by the local Home Guard. Other patrols were involved in this night exercise and the assembly point for the Auxiliaries was near Leominster, before they were transported to their start point, nearer the viaduct. This meeting place for the Auxiliaries was almost certainly Eye Manor, the home of Captain Sandford, the IO for the two counties after John Todd. Colin almost made it to the objective and was crawling along a ditch within yards of the viaduct, when he was spotted by a Home Guardsman. Years later, one of these ex-Home Guards, by coincidence, came to live in the Lenches and when asked by Colin, remembered the exercise and being called out to do a night guard on the viaduct — much to his annoyance!

After all these years, it is impossible to say whether this last scheme was in fact part of a competition for the various Auxiliary patrols. These were introduced in the Winter of 1941/42 by the Headquarters staff at Coleshill, presumably to maintain the interest and morale of the Auxiliaries. It must have occurred to many members of the patrols that there was not now likely to be an invasion of Britain, while Hitler was occupied with his attack on Russia, and that their continuing intensive training might be in vain. Competitions would be a good means of maintaining efficiency and enthusiasm, and were arranged by the Group Leaders on a county-wide basis initially, to establish county champions, with semi-finals and finals being organised by the HQ Staff and held at Coleshill. A second series of competitions were held at Coleshill during the Autumn of 1942, with a third series after the harvest in 1943. The influence of the farmers amongst the Auxiliers was probably a factor here!

In Worcestershire, the county trials were normally conducted at Wolverton Hall where a number of the ex-Auxiliaries remember going and meeting other patrols for practice in rifle shooting, grenade throwing and explosives tests. For these the Auxiliaries would be accommodated in the outbuildings during their stay at the hall. Competitions were also held in Herefordshire in which the Worcestershire men participated, and it seems that Holmer was the base for these tests. A number of patrols from the two counties made it to the semi-finals and finals at Coleshill, including the men from Claines, Crowle and Broadheath.

Typically the tests for the Auxiliaries in the competitions involved:

1) The No.36 grenade—throwing this into a metal container from different ranges.

2) Night firing with the .22 rifle.

3) Efficiency Race, which in fact was a relay race against the clock, involving each member of the patrol, in turn, negotiating obstacles and carrying out a number of tasks. The latter included revolver firing at a target and dismantling and assembling a grenade. This sort of physical exercise obviously favoured the younger men and is perhaps the reason why the boy scouts from Broadheath were so successful in competitions.

4) Providing a number of solutions to explosives problems.

5) The main event of the competition would be a night patrol to a target. Typically this would involve the Auxiliary patrols carrying out a daytime reconnaissance to establish their routes to the objective. This could be perhaps a lorry parked near Coleshill, to which they would be required to make their way, using their night operational skills, and affix magnets without being seen and apprehended by the guards. For the exercise the patrols would be taken some distance away by lorry and have to make their way back to the objective on foot and by crawling. A large element of luck as well as skill was needed to compete successfully in this part of the competition, as will be seen below.

A number of the Auxiliaries from Worcestershire remember the competitions and particularly the last exercise. John Boaz of Samson Patrol recalls:

We met all the patrols led by the van Moppes in local competitions. We won these and went on to compete against the patrols from Herefordshire and Monmouthshire. After winning these local competitions we went down to Coleshill for the semi-finals against six other patrols from other parts of the UK, which we won again. Later, we returned to Coleshill for the final. One patrol, I remember, came from Kent, who won it and another from the Borders area. We came third as a result of some bad luck.

One of the tests was a night operation, where each of the patrols had to reach a target and return in one hour. Each patrol was told where the target was and given an hour in the afternoon to find it and work out their plans for the coming night. We were told that there would be two trip wires within so many hundreds of yards of the start with a sentry and then some more trip wires within a few hundred yards of the finish, with two sentries. We worked out our approach to the target, utilising a ditch and some large bushes, through which we made a track that we would recognise in the dark. Most of our training had been for this sort of operation and we felt pretty confident about it.

On the night we had negotiated all the hazards and were close to completion when a local searchlight came on and exposed us. In these circumstances we were trained to 'freeze' and not move. One of the sentries spotted us and he was duly knocked over, during the course of which he cut his leg and had to go to hospital. But for us the game was up. It was bad luck that a local searchlight, which was nothing to do with Coleshill and was probably illuminating the night sky for a German aircraft, came to be activated. As a result of being 'exposed' in this way we failed this test and came third overall. I am sure we would have won otherwise.

Other tests included the use of explosives and grenade throwing into a tin box about ten feet square from various distances. We were pretty good at this.

After the competition, we went to the Officers' Mess for drinks and we palled up with the patrol from the Borders. One of them had postponed his wedding to compete in the finals at Coleshill and needless to say too much was drunk! I remember this man having to be carried back to our billets.

On another occasion at Coleshill, I remember that one of the tests involved crossing a lake with a temporary raft made of oil drums and that when we were about halfway across the officers exploded a bomb and pitched us into the lake!

A similar test to this latter one, described by John, is remembered by others as being rigged up at Holmer. Perhaps this was to provide practice for the competitions at Coleshill?

Jim Holt remembered going to Coleshill for competitions and recalls aspects of the competitions there:

It was winter and our objective was a lorry parked inside a high wall at Coleshill, where we were to place magnets. We had previously been warned by Roger Smith that there was snow on the ground and so we took white overalls for this exercise. We were told where the objective was and allowed to recce the approach during the day. During the night approach one of our patrol managed to reach the objective by crawling along the top of the wall but I was hiding in the ruts of a cart track when I was trodden on by a guard and captured. I was the only one caught on this exercise and the patrol came second as a result. But for this, I think we would have won!

John Wythes remembers that his patrol went to Coleshill a number of times and did win one of the competitions but could not remember which. Dick Philips also recalls going down to compete and although his patrol did not win, he thought that they had held their own against the others.

During the summer of 1944 and after the period of guard duty by the Auxiliaries on the Isle of Wight, it was now considered by the HQ Staff to be unreasonable for patrols competing in competitions to make the journey down to Coleshill. So a series of 'circus' visits by the Headquarters Training Staff were made to the various operational areas. Six were apparently made during June/July of that year, when the training staff took along suitable equipment for the exercises. The Monmouthshire Auxiliaries remember that Colonel Douglas, who was by this time the Commanding Officer at Coleshill, attended their demonstration, and it is likely that he was also at the demonstration put on by Samson Patrol from Broadheath and remembered by John Boaz.

I remember on one occasion, the van Moppes 'phoning up to say some officers were coming up from Coleshill and could we put on a demonstration of our skill at reaching a target unseen. The target was a pile of five gallon petrol cans set up in a field, near Knightwick, I think, and we were to place some magnets on them. We were told beforehand where the target would be and the officers wanted to observe our progress from a nearby road. The start point was about a mile away. Val Clines, the Sergeant, suggested that we should surprise the officers in some way and I suggested that we borrow a big old Austin car and an old-fashioned farm trailer from my uncle, who lived close by. We did this and fitted wooden slats across the top of the solid side boards of the trailer and covered this with straw. While the rest of the patrol climbed into the trailer and hid in the space underneath the straw, I put on an old farm smock and some glasses. I put the magnets in my top pocket and then drove to the field with the target, past the officers waiting on the roadside. They acknowledged my wave as I went by. When I stopped in the gateway, I could see that the farmer had put some cattle in the field since we had first seen the target but I was able to use this to my advantage. When I slowly walked into the field the cattle became excited and milling round, followed me up to the drums. Here I was able to drop the magnets out of my top pocket and kick them up against the drums. Afterwards I returned to the car and drove back to the start, again waving to the waiting officers.

When we got back to the start point Val Clines said he thought we should now do the exercise properly. We put on our denims and started to work our way back to the target, crawling where necessary. We could see the officers still standing on the roadside and when we got within a couple of hundred yards of the target, they came into the field and congratulated us on our progress. Val Clines was able to say to them that this was in fact the second time we had visited the field. Naturally the officers did not believe us until they walked up to the petrol cans and could see the magnets. They were impressed and invited us up to the Talbot at Knightwick for a drink with them but first we had to collect the car and trailer. The patrol climbed into the trailer again and I put on my disguise before driving to the Talbot. I could see the officers standing outside, waiting for us to arrive, but again they did not recognise me when I drew up outside. Not until the back of the trailer had been dropped and the patrol climbed out did the officers realise what had happened earlier. At this point the officers said that the patrol deserved two pints each. I am sure that if this exercise had been for real we could have blown up the target and got away without being caught!

This exercise amply illustrates the degree of skill in field craft and initiative of which the Auxiliaries were capable when operating on their own ground. The fact that they had fooled their training officers during the hours of daylight suggests that the force would have had even greater success operating at night against German occupation forces. Some Auxiliaries have even expressed the view that they were disappointed that the Germans did not invade Britain— they wanted to use their skills and equipment as intended. This attitude indicates the generally high level of morale and confidence the Auxiliaries had.

CHAPTER 10
Individual Urban Saboteurs

There is evidence from the Birmingham area that individual Home Guard saboteurs were recruited and this may provide an alternative explanation for the OBs in and around Worcester. A former member of the Birmingham Home Guard who wishes to remain anonymous tells of his recruitment to such an urban guerrilla force:

> I was a Corporal in a works Home Guard in the Birmingham area, when I was told to report to the Battalion Headquarters. Here I was introduced to a Lieutenant who questioned me at length about the reasons for my turning down offers of further promotion. He then asked me if I was interested in joining a special unit called 'X Branch', which would require extra training and for me to go on various courses. The thought of doing something more exciting appealed to me and, after more discussion, I agreed to join.
>
> One of the residential courses I went on was to Altcar, where ostensibly I was to do Lewis gun training. In fact the course was much more extensive and included fieldcraft, bombing and making up demolition sets. Other people on the course included Home Guardsmen from South Wales and Regular Army troops, including officers. All of us were referred to as students by the instructors and treated as equals. As the only Corporal on the course, I was the lowest rank there and was very pleased with this arrangement. The course finished with each student giving a lecture to the rest of the class on a specific item that we had been taught. I managed to pass out in the highest category (AX), entitling me to carry out live bombing practices and, after adequate training to qualify other Home Guard personnel to do the same. I was further qualified to carry out the mandatory destruction of any unexploded bombs and grenades after live practice. I was subsequently told by HQ that, in the event of an invasion, I was to destroy my certificate, to avoid my being identified as a member of the Home Guard with special skills.
>
> On other residential courses I had been taught how to make up demolition sets from four No. 73 Grenades (a.k.a. the Thermos Flask Granade)

taped round a central detonator. Together these added up to 18 pounds of nitro-glycerine explosive. I had also been trained in the making of booby traps and the skills of dirty fighting, including the use of a knife.

My only contact with the shadowy X Branch was the previously mentioned Lieutenant, whom I would meet from time to time at the HQ for instructions. I was expected to train and operate alone and generally keep a low profile within my more general Home Guard duties. It was rather like the French Resistance, where one would work alone and be controlled by one officer. I do not know of anyone else who was recruited by X Branch, although there must have been others in my area. Information was only divulged on a 'need to know' basis.

Had there been an invasion, I would have been contacted and told to report to Cockshoot Hill School in Birmingham, the mustering point for other Home Guardsmen, in addition to those in X Branch. There I would be told what I was expected to do and where our underground ammunition and food stores had been established. I was aware that such bunkers existed but not where, as part of the secrecy which surrounded the X Branch organisation.

I was advised by my X Branch Lieutenant to practise operating at night, alone, which involved dressing in civilian 'mufti', including rubber soled shoes and walking through the blacked-out streets, which besides developing my night vision would also develop a sixth sense for when I was about to walk into a lamp post or step off a kerb! I was also advised to try the exercise running, which I found to be particularly nerve-wracking. I was to practise 'freezing', which involved standing absolutely still. After the continual nightly air raids on Birmingham had abated there was only sporadic activity. Shortly after the pubs had shut at 10 p.m., the only people about were police on patrol and Air Raid Wardens, so the risk of discovery was minimal. However, it was necessary to have a plausible reason for being abroad at this time of night (visiting a married girl friend) and for being in hiding (needing to urinate).

Face blacking was not to be used. If necessary, a dark, lightweight scarf could be used for cover, as this could be quickly pulled down and appear to be normal dress.

Another skill in which I was trained was the manufacture of my own explosives, utilising nitric acid and sulphuric acid in approximately equal parts and cotton waste, or the use of various mixtures of saltpetre, fertilizer, weedkiller and sugar. In the industrial midlands, the acids were widely used in the manufacture of car batteries and for cleaning metal castings. They were therefore not a problem to procure.

I was also advised to brush up on my Morse Code and even now I can remember the Morse for my code name, which was 'Charlie', although I have forgotten the rest.

All equipment, although effective, was to be seen to be home-made and thus untraceable. I was not issued with a Fairbairn-Sykes knife. I had to make my own from a broken or worn power hacksaw blade, which were in plentiful supply at my works and were made of really good, two inch wide, hardened steel. This would be ground to a Bowie-like profile and provided with a wooden handle, bolted through the ready-made hole in the end of the former hacksaw blade. The quality steel would take a really keen edge on a whet-stone. The scabbard for my knife was made of leather from an old school satchel and provided with two wide elastic bands to fix it to my leg. This could be discretely hidden under my trouser leg but nevertheless the knife could be drawn quickly with one hand.

I also made myself a garrotting wire from a cheese wire supplied to me and two home made wooden 'tee-piece' handles. I was told that with this device it was possible to decapitate a man, silently! I was also supplied with two practice hand grenades with which I was to devise various forms of booby-trap. These were purposely to be my own design so that the Germans would not be aware of any standard pattern of trap and so be less able to disarm them. There would normally be two traps in sequence, one fairly obvious, the other much less so to trap the unwary!

The one exception to home-made equipment was a demolition timer. A cord fuse was suitable for only short delays. As improvised timing devices had proved to be unreliable, I was issued with a timer. This consisted of a fully jewelled precision clock movement with a dial on one end, which could be set for delay time. After the expiry of this time, a spring-loaded plunger was released, which closed a pair of electrical contacts. A built-in safety device prevented premature operation. The timer was designed to plug into a small three pin socket which was wired into the demolition set. It was intended that the timer would be carried separately and plugged in at the last moment. This reduced the amount of time when there was a risk of discovery.

The conclusion to be reached from the foregoing is that the urban Home Guard saboteurs were to work in an entirely different way to their country cousins in the GHQ Auxiliaries. They were, however, to have been provided with hidden caches of munitions. Were such people recruited and trained in Herefordshire and Worcestershire and could this account for the additional underground stores in and around Worcester? Certainly, Lord Bridgeman, who was appointed to the post of Director General of the Home Guard in 1941, was a keen advocate of of a guerrilla role for the force and his ideas were taken up by some local commanders. He was aware of the Russian propensity for sabotage activities behind the lines and thought the Home Guard were suited to this role. His critics considered that his ideas could compromise the Auxiliary Units and probably confuse the regular Home Defence troops. Since General Montgomery also proposed that the Home Guard, as well as regular troops, should develop a more offensive stance and adopt all forms of fighting, it is quite feasible that the Worcester Battalion commanders could have been inspired by these leaders to have formed their own stay behind force. It would be interesting to know if anyone recalls such people being recruited and trained in Worcester.

CHAPTER 11
Special Duties Section

There was another clandestine organisation, recruited largely but not exclusively from civilians, whose role was to collect information on the presence of German invasion units in Britain and to transmit this intelligence by written message and radio, in stages, to GHQ Home Forces. This intelligence organisation was called Special Duties Section, another deliberately obscure name chosen to give no indication of its actual role.

Although now released from their Official Secrets Act commitments, civilian participants in this spying organisation have been even more reticent than their GHQ Auxiliary Unit colleagues to come forward and tell us their stories. However, there are enough clues and contacts for the authors to be confident that such an organisation existed in the counties of Herefordshire and Worcestershire. Few primary source documents have been released by the government's Military Intelligence services to the Public Record Office which relate to the Special Duties Section, and those that do relate primarily to their HQ, which was also at Coleshill. A degree of speculation is therefore inevitable in our analysis of the available evidence but hopefully it will jog a few memories and perhaps encourage some of the former 'spies' to tell come forward and tell more.

The first public acknowledgement that such an organisation existed was made in *War Illustrated* in 1945 but this appears to have been largely forgotten until 1968 when David Lampe in his book, *Last Ditch*, dealt with the transfer of ATS officers to Special Duties to operate some of the radio stations from 1942 onwards. An article in the November 1996 issue of the Defence of Britain Project newsletter, *Defence Lines*, written by the late Arthur Gabbitas, provided corroboration for much of what David Lampe had said about the way the Special Duties Section radio network was organised. Arthur Gabbitas was, however, speaking from first hand experience since he was a member of the Royal Corps of Signals, serving with the Signals Section at Coleshill during the period that the Special Duties Section was based there.

Arthur Gabbitas told us that wireless networks were established in broadly the same areas as those of the GHQ Auxiliary Units. Here Control Zero radio stations were set up, each one covering an area the size of a county. The Royal Signals and Auxiliary Territorial Service (ATS) radio operators were provided with camouflaged underground radio stations, not unlike the operational bases provided for the Auxiliaries. These underground facilities were normally close to an above ground military signals establishment and would be equipped with stores for a month, together with cooking, sleeping and toilet facilities. Although it is not clear where he obtained his information, David Lampe says that the control stations were also intended to be established within the perimeter of Divisional HQs, which may be significant for our area of study.

Arthur Gabbitas also told us about some of the details of a Control Zero station. These would incorporate a sealed chamber which contained a battery charger, an essential requirement because the wireless sets were in constant use. The generator used to charge the batteries also provided power for the lighting and air conditioning, the exhaust gasses from the motor driving the generator being extracted through a long tunnel which doubled as an emergency escape route. The aerial system for these stations was directional, constructed from copper wire and about 70 feet long. To help disguise its presence the aerial would be strung in a high tree and the connecting cable normally concealed in the bark of the tree trunk by grooving the trunk and covering the cable with plaster painted to match the bark. The high frequency, low powered, signal from the 6 volt radio would normally be sufficient to reach the horizon but this could be extended by siting the station on high land.

To operate the Control Zero stations throughout those parts of Britain where the Special Duties organisation was established seemingly involved some 60 or so Royal Signals men and 43 women ATS officers who were selected and trained at Coleshill. Beatrice Temple, the niece of the then Archbishop of Canterbury, commanded the latter. One of those ATS officers was Edwina Burton, now living in Malvern, who has related her experiences as a Control Zero radio operator. Although this duty was carried out in Kent, her memories of the 18 months spent there do give a first hand account of the way this part of the system was organised and manned.

Miss Burton spent that time operating a radio in a heavily camouflaged underground facility to the north of Harrietsham. This was located in a small woodland, on a hillside forming part of the North Downs and overlooking the main A20 from Folkestone to London. The radio hide apparently still exists and has been found by fellow researchers. The brick-built structure was entered by a vertical shaft, utilising a steel ladder to climb in and out, much like an Auxiliary patrol OB. Miss Burton's radio duty was shared by another ATS girl and their activities were controlled by a Royal Signals captain and small staff

The GHQ Home Forces shoulder patch, worn by Special Duties Section ATS radio operators. (Mick Wilks collection)

occupying a large house nearby. Her radio hide was fitted with two camp beds for use by the operators and they were provided with a supply of food and water. Miss Burton thought the radio supplied for their use was the fairly standard British Army No.17 R/T set and there is evidence from Auxiliary Unit files at the Public Record Office that indicates a large number of this type of radio were ordered by the HQ Staff at Coleshill as a result of requests by Intelligence Officers. The aerial for the Harrietsham station was indeed fixed in the branches of a nearby tall tree, with the connecting wires carefully hidden within the bark of the tree trunk.

Edwina Burton probably owes her transfer to Special Duties Section as a radio operator to the fact that her sister was the civilian secretary to Major Petherick, MP, who was part of the Special Duties staff at Coleshill. It seems likely therefore that recommendation and personal contact influenced recruitment of ATS operators to the Special Duties staff, like the civilian Auxiliary Operational Unit recruits, rather than simply transfer from general duties. Miss Burton's induction to this clandestine radio service followed an interview with a Captain Jones of the Royal Signals at Coleshill. Other Special Duties officers she recalls meeting at Coleshill were Captain Kirkness and Major Childe.

Miss Burton's initial radio training was also conducted at Coleshill where the ATS operators were rather disparagingly known as the Secret Sweeties. During her time there, she and other ATS trainees were billeted at Hannington Hall, situated about two miles to the west of Highworth. Contrary to a widely held view, Hannington Hall was not the headquarters of Special Duties Section, but the home of Mr and Mrs Fry, who continued to live there, with the remainder of the house used primarily as a billet for Royal Signals' officers. Apparently the only office there was that of the ATS adjutant. The HQ for Special Duties Section was at Coleshill to which Edwina Burton, the other trainees and staff officers would travel each day.

Part of Miss Burton's training included firing weapons for which she went to Thetford Forest and was accommodated in a small Nissen hut. Here she experienced live firing with rifle, revolver and sub-machinegun. For her, the rifle and revolver firing was not a success, the latter being particularly difficult to control due to the kick, but she found the automatic weapon, probably a Sten,

Hannington Hall, near Highworth, the wartime billet for Special Duties Section staff and trainee signals officers. (Mick Wilks collection)

to be much more to her liking—spraying the target with bullets from this weapon was altogether more successful!

After training, Edwina Burton's 18 months of duty at the Harrietsham Control Zero station, awaiting the invasion that never came, was punctuated only by visits from Royal Signals personnel to change the radio batteries and to check that the radio was functioning properly. Practise transmissions to South-East Command, Home Forces, involved reciting various passages of text. Strangely, for a clandestine radio system, no coding of messages was involved nor was Morse used. Some time in 1944 and after the German V1 Flying Bomb campaign had started, Miss Burton was transferred back to ATS general duties; she recalls the V1s over-flying her radio bunker while in Kent.

Through Geoff Devereux, we have also made contact with another member of Special Duties Section, Bert Davies, now living in Dawlish, who was also based at Coleshill. He has given us a further insight to life at the headquarters and how the radio network was established. Bert confirms some of what Edwina Burton has told us about Coleshill and adds more detail about the construction of radios there, and the establishment and operation of radio stations in South Wales and near the south coast. Unfortunately he was unable to enlighten us about the location of radio stations in Herefordshire and Worcestershire.

Bert was posted to Coleshill, along with two other men, after an intensive six month radio course at Rugby Technical College, ostensibly to prepare them for radar operation. At Coleshill, the three radio mechanics were accommodated with other Royal Signals staff in three Nissen huts in a wooded part of the grounds. On arrival, the newcomers were made aware that they were something special, since in six years of Army life, none of them had come to a new billet with ready-made beds, sandwiches and a flask of hot drink awaiting them.

Bert was not aware of Hannington Hall being associated with Special Duties staff. He remembers the officers and their mess being in Coleshill House. As for the Signals staff, their mess was in the outbuildings at Coleshill and two of their three Nissen huts were used as recreation rooms, one containing an old piano, the other a moth-eaten snooker table. These items were their prime means of entertainment, except on one memorable occasion when an ENSA concert party found Coleshill by mistake. They were looking for a nearby RAF Station but were persuaded to stop and give the Coleshill staff a show. One of the entertainers was Charlie Chester, later of radio fame.

Major Green was the Signals' CO, with Sergeant Webb and Corporals Higgins and Bartholomew in charge of the Signals' huts. There would be about a dozen Signals' men at any one time at Coleshill, the rest being out working as teams setting up and maintaining Control Zero and Outstation radios elsewhere in the country. Above their living hut, a large overhanging branch of a tree was chained-up to prevent it falling on to their roof, but apart from that worrying feature of their life there, Bert recalls that Coleshill in the summer was a really beautiful location at which to be working.

While at Coleshill, Bert and his fellow radio mechanics were involved in the assembly of the small civilian TRD Outstation radios. These were about 8 inches x 8 inches x12 inches in size and powered by one 6 volt accumulator. Each set was assembled individually—there was no production line, as has been said elsewhere. Apparently the sets were of a very simple design and Bert can recall that one of the components, all of which were civilian supply, was a red cylinder that produced a hissing noise when activated. The aerial cable for the radios was also formed at Coleshill and incorporated a Paxolin core (a sort of early plastic for insulation). This was quite a laborious process until Bert redesigned the cable to omit the Paxolin. This considerably eased their assembly and reduced the amount of material used.

Bert was also involved in the installation of both Control Zero and the Outstation radios in two areas: South Wales and between Taunton and the Isle of Wight. For this task the Signals' men from Coleshill would go out in teams of three or four with an officer in charge, a sergeant, a radio mechanic and sometimes an assistant. To carry their equipment they would have an Austin 8 Utility pickup with a canvas covered back. Bert would usually travel separately by motorcycle. He can recall on one occasion, and probably the only time he came to Worcestershire during the war, stopping to pick up plums in the Vale of Evesham, on their way from Coleshill to South Wales. They were invited by the kindly orchard owner to take as many as they wanted. They filled up the back of the 'Tilly' until the springs were fully compressed!

During the times when they were out fitting or maintaining radios, the team would not stop for more than a week in any particular locality and would arrange their own billets. The team workshop at one time was established in an empty shop in Fisherton Street, Salisbury. Bert remembers that the underground Control Zero radio stations were not always very sophisticated structures but that there would be an escape tunnel for the radio operators should they be discovered. He can recall fitting some of the cabling in the tunnels and stringing aerials in tall trees. For this latter purpose they preferred a beech tree since it was easier to sink the aerial cables into the bark and camouflage them, achieved by using a putty filler and grey/green paint to finish off. This information is consistent with that given by Arthur Gabbitas and Edwina Burton.

Stringing aerials in trees caused quite a number of casualties amongst Bert's colleagues. They were provided with climbing ropes and these would normally be carried in the back of the 'Tilly' along with the acid filled accumulators. Inevitably there would be some acid spillage and this would attack the ropes, weakening them, and cause them to fail when in use. Bert was himself lucky to survive a fall when the branch he was sitting on snapped and he only just managed to grab a rope and pull himself upright before hitting the ground!

Bert confirms that the civilian radios were usually operated by vicars, doctors and vets and he remembers sets being installed near St Davids, Pembrokeshire; at Haverfordwest—this one in a boatyard, near a creek; at Camarthen, in a shop opposite a pub; and another at The Mumbles, near Swansea. One of the sets which he was involved with was operated by a vicar and installed in a garden cold frame on the Isle of Wight. Bert recalls that this vicar was not at all hospitable and the team had to sleep in a nearby hay barn which was particularly uncomfortable.

Bert also confirms that, while radio messages should have been encrypted using the standard Army code sheets, most were in fact sent in 'plain' language, which fits with what Edwina Burton has said. He cannot remember meeting any of the ATS operators at Coleshill but that there were some at a Control Zero Station located in a copse overlooking Salisbury Racecourse. Here there was an above ground small Nissen hut and the underground chamber, about 8 feet square, was constructed from railway sleepers. Access to the latter was via a camouflaged trap door in the centre of a large sawn-off tree stump.

Unfortunately no direct evidence of a Control Zero radio station being sited in Herefordshire or Worcestershire has so far been discovered but the authors have been investigating likely locations. Three possibilities exist but nothing has yet been proved. The strongest candidate comes from evidence found on local Home Guard records that there was a Royal Signals' unit occupying Park

Attwood, a large house occupying high land a couple of miles to the north-west of Kidderminster. Another Royal Signals' camp and radio station was established at Pulley Lane, to the south of Droitwich. Either could have incorporated a stay behind underground bunker. A third possibility lies in the vicinity of Whitney-on-Wye, in west Herefordshire, for the 2nd London Brigade, who were then part of the Western Command reserve, established a headquarters at Whitney Court during 1940 and it would be essential for there to have been a signals' facility. A Control Zero station to receive 'intelligence' about German invasion forces entering England from Wales, perhaps sited in the woods overlooking the main A438 from Wales and the two former railway lines through the Wye valley here would therefore be a distinct possibility.

Two clandestine radio facilities have come to light in Worcester itself as a result of the Defence of Britain Project work: one located in an air raid shelter-like building alongside the canal near the former brickworks at Gregory's Bank, St Georges Lane North; the other in a brick-built building behind a house in Malvern Road, St John's. The former radio station by the canal was apparently to be manned by the then headmaster of the Worcester Royal Grammar School, Mr Pullinger, and the County Council's Director of Education after an invasion and would have been the main means of broadcasting in the locality should the area have been cut off by the invading forces. These two gentlemen were apparently chosen because their voices would have been recognised by the listeners as not being German 'plants' and that their messages were genuine. This building has only recently been demolished. The building used as a radio station in St John's and its aerial still exist and it is said it was used for contact with the wartime Polish resistance. But were these in fact part of the

The former canalside radio station near St George's Lane North in Worcester in the centre of the picture. The building has now been demolished.
(Colin Jones)

Special Duties radio network for this area? Would these radios have been used to maintain contact from the besieged city with the Auxiliaries and the regular Home Defence forces assembling for a counter-attack?

It is possible too, that the radio operated by Captain Sandford at Eye Manor may have had a Special Duties function as well as being used to maintain contact with Coleshill. Use as Special Duties radio stations may also account for some of the OB-like structures discovered in Worcestershire but which are not associated with the known Auxiliary patrols.

Arthur Gabbitas tells us that should an invasion have occurred, the above ground signals staff would have left the area when threatened by enemy forces, leaving the ATS or Royal Signals' radio operators hidden in their underground radio bunker to carry on manning their set. From there they would continue to relay intelligence to a GHQ Home Forces receiving station, until they were either captured or they managed to escape when discovered by the enemy. They most certainly would have been, sooner or later, for the Gestapo became quite proficient at tracking SOE radio operators in occupied France later in the war. Miss Burton thought that her ATS uniform, and the fact that the radio operators were not armed, despite their earlier weapons training, might have prevented them from being shot. However, their treatment by the Germans after capture would not have been at all kindly, and ATS operators would almost certainly have been tortured to find out as much as possible about the intelligence gathering system.

Incoming information to the Control Zero Stations was from civilian operated radio Outstations. Bert Davies has told us how these simple, low-powered radio sets were hidden in a variety of locations. The civilian operators were recruited secretly by a local Special Duties Section Intelligence Officer and came from all walks of life. Bert has mentioned doctors, vicars and vets, but shopkeepers, farmers and even housewives were also apparently recruited. Again, the authors have unearthed no direct evidence of Outstations in the two counties, yet there must have been since there is evidence of a complimentary spying system having been established in Worcestershire, as will be shown below.

Just over the border, in Monmouthshire, George Vater, a retired farmer who was recruited to Special Duties as a message carrier, in 1941, has described how he was recruited and how the civilian part of the 'intelligence' gathering system was organised. Living in the area just to the east of Abergavenny, part of George's role as a courier or 'cut-out', as they were then called, was to pick up messages from a number of 'dead letter drops' and deliver these to his local vicar. The vicar would then relay the contents by radio to a Control Zero station which was located on the Blorenge, a hill to the south of Abergavenny, from where the messages would be radioed to the local Western Command HQ. Incidentally, one of the officers at the Royal Signals' HQ in Abergavenny was

George Vater in October 2000 with the map issued to him by 'Tommy Atkins' in 1941. (Mick Wilks)

Major Andrew Cruickshank, who was later to take the part of the elderly doctor in the television series, 'Doctor Finlay's Casebook'. Bert Davies remembers that the Blorenge underground facility was created by enlarging an existing rock cave using explosives and was quite surprised to find that parts of the structure still existed—he thought it had been totally destroyed at the end of the war.

George Vater has written down his memories of how he was recruited and the spying system as it was organised in part of Monmouthshire. These are reproduced below and no doubt reflect the method of organising Special Duties operations elsewhere.

On 5th November 1941, I was called for a medical for the army, in Newport, opposite the County Hall building. I think there must have been 30 to 40 young lads to go before the doctors. First we were sat in desks and a paper placed before us by an army sergeant. We had 20 minutes in which to complete this paper, an IQ test. After our medicals, a few of us were told that Colonel Hughes was to interview us. At the end of the interview, I was told that someone would come and see me in the next few days.

Thus came the arrival of a person who identified himself as 'Tommy Atkins', who started to cross-examine me regarding my medical and the interview with the Colonel. I took an Oath of Allegiance and was told I was to do something very secret which meant I was to be sworn to secrecy as no documents or signing of names could be done. I had to swear on a small Bible, held in the hand of 'Tommy Atkins', and this time to repeat after him and swear to abide by the Defence of the Realm Act and the Official Secrets Act. I was now told what was entailed and if the enemy landed, could expect about 14 days' activity—[this is about the life expectancy estimated for the Auxiliary Patrol recruits]. I was then given the names of eight other people who had all been sworn to secrecy. There were three vicars, a doctor, an engineer, a carpenter, a gardener and a farm worker. I was also given a map together with a large amount of edible paper, which was very much like chewing gum when tasted. Also numerous 'Top Secret' documents and lists of German units from Cap Griz Nez to the Hook of Holland. These units, I was told, I had to

125

Former garage for Llanarth vicarage and one of George Vater's dead letter collection points. In this case messages were to be left behind a loose board in one of the garage doors. The building has since been converted to residential use. (Mick Wilks)

learn by heart, together with their colours and insignias, and where they were based. I was told the name of the wireless operator, where to contact him day and night, and where the wireless would be hidden. The operator was the Reverend Sluman of Llantilio Crossenny.

A map was to be used to give pinpoint readings of any enemy forces in our area. The correctness of these references was vital and had to be delivered to 'Tommy Atkins' and later to the radio operator who would transmit them to GHQ Western Command. Each message was timed when passed from one runner to another. By day the observations were made, but the messages were carried during darkness. Also the messages were left in field postboxes. Mine was a tennis ball with a slit in it, prepared and given to me by 'Tommy Atkins'. It was hidden in the bole of a yew tree amongst the dead nettles. At Llanddewi Church, it was a loose stone in the churchyard wall and at Llanarth, behind a loose board, on the door of a barn, opposite the vicarage.

When 'Tommy Atkins' came a second time, about a week later, I had to show him what was to be the position of our local HQ. I had chosen a barn surrounded by a cattle shed wall about 5 feet high and which was approachable from five different roads. He thought it was a good choice due to its high elevation and the fact that it could be arrived at by so many routes and therefore no more than two people need approach from the same direction. I was then tested on how well I could map read and how much of the secret notes I had learnt. The notes were then burnt in his presence.

From George Vater's notes and the subsequent discussions with him it is possible to build up a picture of how the spying system would have been put in place in Herefordshire and Worcestershire. The Intelligence Officer who recruited George was possibly Captain John Todd, although why he should use the soubriquet 'Tommy Atkins', when he was much more open about his name when recruiting Auxiliaries in Worcestershire, is not clear. Perhaps it was because the Abergavenny area was a bit close to home, as George tells us that 'Tommy Atkins' lived at Llanfihangel Crucorny, only a few miles to the north of Abergavenny. His regular appearance in fishing gear and in particular a tweed hat festooned with fishing flies is clearly remembered by George. This has been referred to by others and, although not proof positive, is synonymous with Captain Todd, who was a keen fisherman and apparently something of an eccentric.

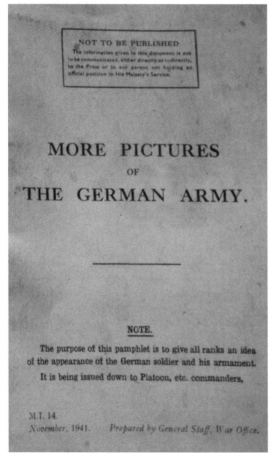

One of the information leaflets issued to the Auxiliaries and Special Duties spies during World War II. (Bernard Lowry collection)

It is also clear that the 'spies' were organised into teams, rather like the Auxiliary patrols of the Operational Branch, each team feeding a radio outstation with intelligence. Should their situation as civilian spies have become untenable after an invasion and occupation by German forces, and their carefully organised message carrying system had broken down, or contact lost with 'Tommy Atkins', then the HQ, as George calls it, would have become the assembly point for the survivors. The isolated and elevated location of the barn chosen for this purpose by George would have at least given them some warning of an impending attack and a chance of escape via one of the several routes identified earlier.

George Vater has subsequently told us that in his tennis ball he could expect to find messages and instructions left

The altar at Llantilio Crossenny Church from below which the
Reverend Sluman operated his radio Outstation. (Mick Wilks)

by 'Tommy Atkins', who would always include the word 'precisely' in his instructions. If this word did not appear then George was to ignore the message as it would not be genuine. On one occasion he left a message that George was to meet him at Llantilio Crossenny Church, which was about five miles on foot from where he lived. Having arrived there George was roundly told off for not reading his message correctly. It had not included the word 'precisely' and George had a wasted a ten mile round trip. A lesson learnt, however!

George mentions a number of the 'dead letter drops' used by his colleagues. Elsewhere in Britain there is evidence that some messages were hidden in hollow gate hinges or behind the numerous horseshoes that used to hang on the outside of farm buildings. Another favourite was behind the small numbered plates on telephone poles which would be rotated to tell the courier whether there was a message behind it or not. If the number was upright, then there was a message; if it was upside down then the 'drop' was empty.

The radio operated by the Reverend Sluman was hidden under the altar of Llantilio Crossenny Church and the aerial clipped to the side of the tower, alongside the lightening conductor. Vicars were frequently used as radio operators elsewhere so it is quite likely that the same sort of arrangements would have prevailed in Herefordshire and Worcestershire.

George Vater says that the coded message to activate the spying system after an invasion had occurred would be: 'The Balloon's Gone Up'—the same as that issued to the Auxiliary patrols.

Evidence that there was a similar spying system in Herefordshire and Worcestershire comes from five sources but our knowledge of the extent and details of the organisation is so far very limited. In Worcestershire, the first evidence that a message carrying system had been organised came from Doctor Tony Barling, the former Sergeant of Jehu Patrol at Alfrick, who told us that his sister, the late Elizabeth Barling, was the courier for his patrol. Had there been an invasion, she would have collected messages from an old metal teapot which was hidden in the hedge alongside the track leading up to Ravenhills Wood from Ravenhills Green, not far from the Fox and Hounds pub. She was to pass the messages to the van Moppes brothers at Wolverton Hall, and presumably would have placed instructions from the van Moppes back in the teapot for Doctor Barling's patrol to collect and act upon. A similar function is also believed to have been performed by Alec Beck's wife for Adam Patrol, to the west of Hereford. John Thornton has told us of the message system for Jacob Patrol, at Bromyard, involving the local schoolmaster, and it is possible to speculate that the HQ he refers to is likely to have been Eye Manor and Captain Sandford.

The fourth source of evidence was a telephone call to the Worcestershire County Archaeological Service from a retired Worcester postman, who declined to give his name because he still felt bound by the Official Secrets Act. He told us that he and five other fellow postmen had been recruited during the war as message carrying couriers for the Auxiliary units. No details were given of the origin or the destination of the messages.

The fifth, and most substantial piece of evidence, came from Geoff Gurney who formerly lived at Duckswich, near Upton-upon-Severn and told us that his late father, Edgar, had been involved with the 'Secret Army'. His father's role was to take messages to a location near Pool House, on the Hanley Road out of Upton. From there they were picked up by someone from Severn Stoke, where there was, perhaps, a radio outstation. Geoff Gurney can recall that his father had sheaves of papers with German tank types and unit markings, together with rolls of rice paper for the messages. Edgar Gurney was the local coal merchant for the Upton area and also ran a smallholding at Duckswich. He used to travel as far afield as Birmingham on business and these trips and his coal delivery rounds would have provided a good cover for his spying activities. Geoff recalls that his father used to disappear about once a week on his clandestine activities and that other people used to visit their house and hold meetings about their activities. All of this evidence points to a spying cell being formed in the Upton area very much like that described by George Vater, but there the trail goes cold.

CHAPTER 12
Conclusions

Would the Auxiliary Units have given a good account of themselves had there been a German invasion of Britain? Winston Churchill certainly thought so, holding the view that 'these units, in the event of an invasion, should prove a useful addition to Britains regular forces ...' and wished to be kept informed of progress in their formation.

Colonel Gubbins, the first commander of the Auxiliaries, thought that they would have justified their existence, although to what extent would have been dependant on the circumstances. Because the Auxiliaries were all volunteers, their existence had cost the country virtually nothing, yet with their arms and training he thought they would have given a good account of themselves in the invasion areas. He recognised that their usefulness would have been shortlived, either because they would have quickly used up their supplies or been hunted down and eliminated.

Peter Fleming was one of the first intelligence officers appointed by GHQ with the task of forming Auxiliary patrols, in his case in perhaps the most critical area: that of XII Corps in Kent and East Sussex. He was of the opinion that they would have struck some useful blows before 'melting away in the white heat of German ruthlessness'. However, he thought that one of their main handicaps would have been a lack of communication between the patrols, the only method available then being messengers moving through the countryside at night. He considered that while there were leaves on the trees, for perhaps six or seven weeks after an invasion in late September, the OBs might not have been found and that to search for them would have involved the Germans in a major effort. Come the winter, low-flying Luftwaffe reconnaissance aircraft would have spotted the Auxiliaries' tracks more readily and they would have been quickly hunted down. He also thought that greater damage to their prospects and morale would have been the inevitable German reprisals on the civilians, possibly their own families, which would have followed the sabotage actions of the patrols. That said, Peter Fleming found it difficult to find fault with Churchill's estimate of Auxiliaries being a useful addition to the regular forces.

Having now talked to a number of the ex-Auxiliaries from the counties of Herefordshire and Worcestershire, the authors are impressed by the almost universal high morale these men and boys had in 1940. Good training, and having the best equipment then available, certainly helped boost their confidence and encouraged their willingness to take on the Germans. Most seem to have enjoyed being in the Auxiliaries and the experience of doing something more exciting than what was offered by the conventional LDV/Home Guard. They were, however, under no illusions about their life-expectancy and most hoped to give a good account of themselves before being caught. The rural character of the two counties, compared with the coastal areas of the south and east of England, would have been an advantage to the majority of the patrols, both in their operational role and as an aid to any attempts to escape, once their OBs had been discovered. It is likely too that after the front line invading troops had passed through the area, the German occupation forces in the west of the country would have been fewer anyway. Should the Germans have discovered their bases, an escape to the Celtic fringe, from where to carry on the fight, would have been feasible for the Herefordshire patrols, if not the westernmost of the Worcestershire men.

How the morale of the local patrols would have been affected when the inevitable reprisals started against people they knew, is difficult to judge. Geoff Devereux remembers that this aspect was a constant worry to him and his patrol and was one reason why their OB was some distance away from Broadheath where most of their families lived. Perhaps when there was little more to lose, the Auxiliaries would have matched the Germans for ruthlessness. They were certainly so encouraged by their trainers.

Assuming the main German invasion forces had indeed been directed to the south-east of England, then any armoured columns probing inland as far as the West Midlands are likely to have been weakened to some degree by the constant harassment of the conventional LDV/Home Guard. Manning their numerous road blocks, despite their poor armaments, they would have provided a means of delaying the Germans in preparation for the counter-attacks by the GHQ Home Forces reserves garrisoned in the Midlands and West of England. The same effect would have been felt by any enemy diversionary attack up the Bristol Channel or through Wales. By the time they had reached their start points for an attack on their primary objective—the armaments and war materials factories of Birmingham, Coventry and the Black Country—the enemy troops would be tired and depleted. What better time for the Auxiliaries of Herefordshire and Worcestershire to start their night attacks on the tank laagers or lorry parks of the troop convoys, resting in the countryside or billeted in the large houses? Any attempts to reinforce the attacking columns by flying in more troops and equipment to the then rudimentary airfields at Shobdon, Perdiswell or Tilesford, could also be frustrated by the Auxiliaries. The loss of their precious and, by this time, declining reserves of Junkers JU 52 transport aircraft, with their backs broken by the strategically placed small charges set by the Auxiliaries, could also be critical at this stage of the campaign. The same could be said of the rail network, which would certainly have been used by the Germans to reinforce and reprovision their troops in this area. Destruction of sections of the system or blocking rail tunnels by the Auxiliaries would have been very disruptive to their supply lines.

Such operations by the Auxiliaries against the German forces could have been a critical factor in the local defences, more so if they were coordinated, but then this was the weakness identified by Peter Fleming. This aspect of the work of Auxiliaries was to be addressed in 1941 by the creation of the information gathering Special Duties Section, with their spies, couriers and radio operators, and the appointment of the Group Leaders—Captains Hall and Lacon for Herefordshire, and the van Moppes brothers and Roger Smith for Worcestershire—tasked to coordinate Group attacks.

It is very likely that at least some of the Auxiliary patrols were part of the carefully worked out plans for defending Worcester and we can only speculate on whether the radio stations, sited within the city, were to be part of the means of telling the Auxiliaries and the regular forces outside Worcester about conditions inside the besieged city.

During the period when the Auxiliaries were undergoing their secret, wide ranging and sometimes dangerous training, many were accused of not doing their bit for the war effort. Having been sworn to secrecy about their activities, they were of course unable to say what they were doing or defend themselves against such criticism. The Claines patrol in particular seems to have suffered this treatment.

John Boaz reminds us that the majority of the Auxiliaries were farmers' sons, who were expected by their fathers to work hard all day, and then had to turn out at nights to carry out their primary field training, sometimes crawling for miles on their stomachs, perhaps until midnight, and then be up again for work early the next morning. It was doubly galling for the patrol from Broadheath to perhaps finish their training early enough to enjoy a well-earned pint at The Plough, only to find that the Royal Artillery regulars from the local searchlight site had been there earlier and had drunk the pub dry! This sort of frustration must have been experienced by many of the other Auxiliaries.

It is ironic too that, unless the Auxiliaries can prove that they also served in the Home Guard over the period 1940 to 1944, they are ineligible for the Defence Medal. The authors hope that by recording the activities of the patrols and listing the members of the British Resistance Organisation in the two counties, this will go some way to righting the sense of injustice felt by some of the surviving ex-Auxiliaries. We hope to make it more widely known, not only what they did in the way of training but also the commitment they made when they became subject to the Official Secrets Act. This was virtually to sign over their lives, and probably those of their families, to protect the British way of life. Had there been a German invasion in 1940 or 1941, then their life expectancy was likely to be quite short. They were under no illusions about this. The authors believe that that sort of courage and the dedication to training, in many cases for the full four years, 1940 to 1944, is to be admired.

On 18 November 1944, General Franklyn, the then Commander-in-Chief of GHQ Home Forces, wrote to Colonel Douglas at Coleshill explaining that in view of the improved war situation, it had been decided by the War Office that

COPY

The Commander,
GHQ Auxiliary Units.

In view of the improved war situation, it has been decided by the War Office that the Operational Branch of Auxiliary Units shall stand down, and the time has now come to put an end to an organisation which would have been of inestimable value to this country in the event of invasion.

All ranks under your command are aware of the secret nature of their duties. For that reason it has not been possible for them to receive publicity, nor will it be possible even now. So far from considering this to be a misfortune, I should like all members of Auxiliary Units to regard it as a matter of special pride.

I have been much impressed by the devotion to duty and high standard of training shown by all ranks. The careful preparations, the hard work undertaken in their own time, and their readiness to face the inevitable dangers of their role, are all matters which reflect the greatest credit on the body of picked men who form the Auxiliary Units.

I should be glad, therefore, if my congratulations and best wishes could be conveyed to all ranks.

(Signed) R.M. Franklyn

General
Commander-in-Chief

GHQ Home Forces.
18th November, 1944.

A copy of the original letter sent by General Franklyn to Colonel Douglas explaining the decision to stand down the Auxiliary Units

From:- Colonel F.W.R. Douglas.

To:- The Members of Auxiliary Units - Operational Branch.

    The War Office has ordered that the Operational side of Auxiliary Units shall stand down! This is due to the greatly improved War situation and the strategic requirements of the moment.

    I realize what joining Auxiliary Units has meant to you; so do the officers under my command. You were invited to do a job which would require more skill and coolness, more hard work and greater danger, than was demanded of any other voluntary organization. In the event of "Action Stations" being ordered you knew well the kind of life you were in for. But that was in order; you were picked men; and others, including myself, knew that you would continue to fight whatever the conditions, with, or if necessary without, orders.

    It now falls to me to tell you that your work has been appreciated and well carried out, and that your contract, for the moment, is at an end. I am grateful to you for the way you have trained in the last four years. So is the Regular Army. It was due to you that more divisions left this country to fight the battle of France; and it was due to your reputation for skill and determination that extra risk was taken - successfully as it turned out - in the defence arrangements of this country during that vital period. I congratulate you on this reputation and thank you for this voluntary effort.

    In view of the fact that your lives depended on secrecy no public recognition will be possible. But those in the most responsible positions at General Headquarters, Home Forces, know what was done; and what would have been done had you been called upon. They know it well, as is emphasized in the attached letter from the Commander-in-Chief. It will not be forgotten.

                                                 (signature)

30 NOV 44
C/o G.P.O. HIGHWORTH,
Nr. Swindon (Wilts).

                           Colonel,
                          Commander,
                       Auxiliary Units.

Colonel Douglas's letter of thanks to all members of Auxilliary Units, following on from General Franklyn's request

the Operational Branch of the Auxiliary Units should be stood down (refer to illustration opposite). He went on to say that due to the secret nature of their duties it would not be possible for them to receive publicity and that the members should consider this to be a matter of special pride. He asked for his congratulations and best wishes to be conveyed to all ranks.

The Auxiliary Units were stood down at the end of November 1944, just as quietly and secretly as they were formed. The members of the patrols received a letter of thanks from Colonel Douglas, the last Commanding Officer at Coleshill, which reiterated that public recognition for what they had done would not be possible. A small shield-shaped lapel badge was the only other tangible memento that they received for their efforts.

*John Thornton (Jacob Patrol) and Jim Griffin
(Jehu Patrol) patrolling again after 60 years
in September 2001 (Mick Wilks)*

APPENDIX
Surviving works from the local Stop-lines

For those readers who are interested in a more detailed explanation of the conventional military defences in the area, it is intended to produce a further volume dealing with that aspect of the 1940s defences and the role of the Home Guard. In the meantime, it is possible to see surviving defence archaeology at a number of the crossing points along the Stop Lines. A good point to view such remains is at Pershore Bridge in Worcestershire, where the County Council have provided some information boards at the picnic site.

Avon Stop-line

Eckington Bridge Picnic Site (SO 922 423). Prefabricated concrete pillbox and spigot mortar mounting and emplacement. The spigot mortar was an aimable anti-tank or anti-personnel device, beloved by the Home Guard and was one example of their so-called sub-artillery.

Pershore Bridge Picnic Site (SO 952 451). Anti-Tank Cylinders (for use in creating a road block), 6 pounder gun emplacement (now converted into a water pumping station), spigot mortar mountings and trench systems. Worcestershire County Council have provided information boards at this site explaining some of the defences of 1940 for this key river crossing.

Offenham Ford (SP 065 471). Pillbox and Anti-Tank Cylinders. The latter are in the river and can only be seen when water levels are low.

Severn Stop-line

Upton upon Severn riverside (SO 850 408). Anti-Tank Cylinders.

Holt Fleet Bridge (SO 825 634). 6 pounder anti-tank gun emplacement, still with the Hotchkiss gun mounting.

Two type 26 pillboxes, Pershore Bridge, c.1944, part of the Avon Stop-line.
These pillboxes were demolished at the end of the war

Teme Stop-line

Near Little Hereford (SO 537 688). Demolished bridge over the River Teme. This former canal bridge was demolished in 1941 but the abutments can still be seen from a public right of way. Local legend has it that the Home Guard were informed that Crete had been invaded by the Germans but had misheard the message and thought that 'Greete had been invaded' and so in a mistaken act of destruction, blew up this redundant canal bridge! Greete is about four miles away to the north-east. It is more likely that Royal Engineers would have demolished the redundant bridge as a precaution against its possible future use by invading forces, but it's a good story!

Eastham (SO 671 675). Anti-Tank Cylinders alongside the unclassified road through the woods.

Stanford Bridge (SO 715 658). Pillbox built into the abutments of the old bridge over the Teme.

Near Ham Bridge (SO 744606). Anti-Tank Cylinders alongside the B4204.

Ankerdine Hill, near Knightwick (SO 739 572. Anti-Tank Cylinders alongside the B4197.

Wye Stop-line

Bridge Sollars (SO 413 426). A rare Norcon concrete round pillbox can just be glimpsed from the roadside in the winter. This is on private land overlooking the bridge, on the east side of the river, and is inaccessible to the public. There is a spigot mortar mounting nearby and on the same private property.

Mordiford (SO 572 373). Loopholed walls in Mordiford Mill, covering the approaches to Mordiford Bridge.

Huntsham Bridge (SO 567 182). Pillbox adjoining the bridge, on the west bank.

Bibliography

A number of books refer to the Auxiliary Units and related subjects and the authors have used the following to provide background information for their study of this resistance organisation in the counties of Hereford and Worcester.

Alexander, C. *Ironsides Line*, West Sussex, 1999

Angell, S. *The Secret Sussex Resistance. 1940 - 1944*, Midhurst, West Sussex, 1996

Beevor, A. and Cooper, A. *Paris after the Liberation 1944 - 49*, London, 1994

Brown, D. *Somerset v Hitler - Secret Operations in the Mendips 1939 - 1945*, Newbury, 1999

Beyts, Brig. G.H.B. *The King's Salt*, 1996

Calvert, M. *Fighting Mad*, London, 1996

Churchill, W.S. T*he Second World War. Vol. II. Their Finest Hour*, London, 1949

Cocks, A.E. *Churchill's Secret Army 1939 - 45 and other recollections*, Lewes, Sussex, 1992

Collier, B. *The Defence of the United Kingdom*, London, 1957

Cox, R. *Operation Sea Lion*, London, 1974

Croft, A. *A Talent for Adventure*, Hanley Swan, Worcestershire, 1991

Cunningham, C. *Beaulieu: The Finishing School for Agents*, London, 1998

Dear, I. *Sabotage and Subversion - The SOE and OSS at War*, London, 1996

Delaforce, P. *Churchill's Secret Weapons*, 1998

Dewing, G. *Suffolk's Secret Army 1940-44*, East Molesey, Surrey, 1996

Fairbairn, Capt. W.E. *All in Fighting 1942*, London, 1942

Fleming, P. *Invasion 1940 - An account of the German preparations and the British countermeasures*, London, 1957

Flook, R. *British and Commonwealth Military Knives*, Shrewsbury, 1999

Foot, M.R.D. *Resistance*, St Albans, 1978

    SOE 1940 - 1946, London, 1984

Highworth Historical Society. *A History of Highworth. Part 2*, Highworth, 1986

    A History of Highworth, Part 3, Highworth, 1992

Hoare, A. *Standing up to Hitler - The Story of Norfolk's Home Guard and Secret Army 1940 - 1944*, Wymondham, Norfolk, 1997

Hogg, I.V. *The Encyclopedia of Infantry Weapons of World War II*, London, 1977

Johnson, D.E. *East Anglia at War 1939 - 1945*, Norwich, 1992

Kelly's Directory for 1937

Kessler, E. *Hitler on the Doorstep - Operation 'Sea Lion'. The German Plan to Invade Britain*, London, 1997

Lampe, D. *The Last Ditch - The secrets of the nationwide British Resistance Organisation and the Nazi plans for the occupation of Britain 1940 - 1944*, London, 1968

Longmate, N. *If Britain had Fallen*, London, 1972

Lorain, P. *Secret Warfare*, London, 1983

Mackenzie, S.P. *The Home Guard - The Real Story of 'Dad's Army'*, Oxford, 1995

Melton, H. Keith *The Ultimate Spy Book*, London, 1996

Oxenden, Major N.V. *Auxiliary Units History and Achievements 1940 - 1944*, Parham, Suffolk, originally 1944

Sarkar, D. *Angriff Westland. Three Battle of Britain air raids through the looking glass*, Worcester, 1994

Tanner, G. *Around Highworth in Old Photographs*, Gloucester, 1991
    Highworth. Towns and Villages of England series, 1993

Thomas, N. *Partisan Warfare 1941 - 45*, London, 1987

Trevor-Roper, H.R. *Hitler's War Directives 1939-1945*, London, 1964

Walker, D.E. *Operation Amsterdam. The most brilliant and daring raid of the war*, 1980

Ward, A. *Resisting the Nazi Invader*, London, 1997

Weale, A. *Secret Warfare*, 1997

West, N. *MI 6. British Secret Intelligence Service Operations*, London, 1983

Wilkinson, P. and Astley J.B. *Gubbins and SOE*, London, 1993

Wills, H. *Pillboxes*, London, 1985

Primary sources of information on the Auxiliary Units were the following Public Record Office files: WO 199/937, WO 199/1955, WO 199/3265, WO 199/3389 (includes the Nominal Rolls) and WO 199/3390. The following radio programmes also provided useful background information: 'The Balloon Has Gone Up!', broadcast on BBC Radio 4 on 17 December 1993, and 'The Hidden Heroes - The Story of the Secret WW II Resistance', broadcast on Radio 4 on 26 September 1998. Articles from various issues of *Loopholes - The Journal of the Pillbox Study Group* provided some information.

Index